The
Good
Campaigns
Guide

NCVO – voice of the voluntary sector

NCVO champions the cause of the
voluntary sector. It believes that the
voluntary sector enriches society and
needs to be promoted and supported.
It works to improve its effectiveness,
identify unmet needs and encourage
initiatives to meet them.

Established in 1919 as the
representative body for the voluntary
sector in England, NCVO now gives
voice to some 850 organisations –
from large, 'household-name' charities
to small self-help groups involved in
all areas of voluntary and social
action. It is also in touch with
thousands of other voluntary bodies
and groups, and has close links with
government departments, local
authorities, the European Union and
the business sector.

The
Good
Campaigns
Guide

BRIAN LAMB

NCVO Publications

Published by
NCVO Publications
(incorporating Bedford Square Press)
imprint of the
National Council for Voluntary Organisations
Regent's Wharf
8 All Saints Street
London N1 9RL

First published 1997

Typeset in Great Britain by GCS
Printed and bound in Great Britain by
Page Brothers, Norwich
Designed by Fiona Keating
Edited by Marta Maretich
Project Manager David Cameron

A catalogue record for this book is available
from the British Library.

ISBN 0 7199 1504 X

Contents

Voluntary organisations form an integral part of what is known as the third sector or Social Economy. Unity Trust Bank strongly supports the work of the Social Economy and is keen to promote greater recognition of the contribution voluntary organisations make to today's society.

Effective communication plays a vital role in the everyday activities of voluntary organisations throughout the UK. Whether an organisation is trying to increase awareness of its work or encourage support of its projects in terms of time or money, the success of each campaign will rely on how well the message is communicated to the target audience.

Unity Trust Bank is pleased to support *The Good Campaigns Guide* to help voluntary organisations make the most effective use of their resources to successfully achieve a 'good campaign'.

Sir Dennis Landau
Chairman, Unity Trust Bank

UNITY TRUST BANK

Acknowledgements

As usual with a project of this kind, there are too many debts to acknowledge them all. However, I would like to thank Jim Minton of NCVO, who conducted the interviews for the case studies and chased other contributions, and all the organisations which agreed to be interviewed for the case studies. I would also like to acknowledge the contributions of some of those who regularly attend the NCVO Political Activities group, especially Mike Parkinson from Oxfam, Adrian Penrose from RSPB, Janet Morrison and Lindsay Driscoll, both of whom were formerly with NCVO, and Lord Dubs, former Director of the Refugee Council and Adam Gaines of NCVO all of whom helped in various ways to move ideas of good campaigning forward.

My appreciation also goes to Scope for having the foresight to let me undertake this project and to Scope's Public Affairs team for their insights into the campaigning process and their support.

Finally, I would like to thank Hilary, for her support and insights into the complexity of campaigning in an international context, and Rachael and Rebecca, who can now stop asking if it's finished.

The last decade has brought dramatic changes to campaigning organisations and the political environment in which they operate. This has been reflected in the changing context of the legal requirements and guiding principles that govern campaigning. Ideas about what constitutes good campaigning have also been developing but without any consensus about what makes good campaign practice.

The Good Campaigns Guide aims to explore what is currently accepted as best practice among campaigning organisations in the voluntary sector and the ways in which these standards could be developed. It is based on a survey of projects which were undertaken by a number of the leading campaign organisations including Shelter, the RSPCA, Amnesty International, Oxfam and Greenpeace. Interviews were conducted with these organisations and case studies have been compiled to illustrate key lessons for successful campaigning. Evidence was also gathered from other established campaigning organisations and from the discussions of a group of campaign managers who met to share their experiences (see Appendix 2). The guide also draws on the insights offered by academic studies of campaigning.

The Good Campaigns Guide is relevant to organisations of all sizes in the voluntary sector and is designed as a resource for campaigners facing particular issues. It is not designed as a 'how to' manual in the sense of 'how to lobby your MP' or 'how to use petitions'. There are already some excellent books available for those who wish to know more about parliamentary procedure, or general campaigning techniques and some of these are listed in Appendix 4.

The principles that underpin good practice in campaigning are applicable to all organisations and, while some may have particular relevance for campaigners and campaign managers in the voluntary sector, most of these principles will apply to anyone working in a campaigning organisation.

A Definition of Campaigning

What are campaigning activities? The terms 'campaigning' and 'lobbying' have developed negative connotations within modern usage because of the controversy surrounding abuses of the political system. Other words have been advanced to cover these activities, including 'advocacy'. Campaigning retains a common currency that the other words do not and for this reason it seems sensible to continue with its usage. Nevertheless, it is helpful to define the different activities that attach to these terms:

Campaigning is the activity of seeking to bring public pressure to bear on institutions and individuals so that they act differently than they would otherwise have done without the influence of the campaign.
Lobbying is used more narrowly to refer to the attempt to influence elected representatives within the formal democratic system of government, often as part of a more general campaign for change.
Advocacy refers to the pursuit of a particular issue by an individual or organisation on another's behalf, normally within the established framework of law or social entitlements, with the aim of achieving the best outcome.

Organisations carry out activities under a number of headings, including campaigning, advocacy, public-policy work, lobbying, education and issue management. The crucial point is that there are a number of activities that fall within a spectrum which extends from negotiation at one end to aggressive public campaigning at the other, all of which have a place in the repertoire of campaigning organisations.

Why Campaign?

Campaigning is a process which identifies problems, brings them to the attention of decision makers and the public, and advocates change. Voluntary organisations have a duty to act as a conduit for the views of their members, supporters and the people they serve, and their success or failure has a profound effect upon the lives and interests of those they represent and, ultimately, on the quality of public life and decision making.

People campaign when they wish to influence issues that give them cause for concern or which directly affect them. Examples of successful campaigning – together with a frustration with the traditional channels of political influence – have led more people than ever before to use pressure groups to represent their concerns over everything from the environment to living standards and human rights. Campaigning also brings other benefits to individuals and organisations. For individuals, it can offer hope of personal redress or an opportunity to exercise citizenship or pursue broader moral concerns. Working together with others can also provide a solidarity and common purpose missing from other areas of people's lives. As well as achieving important outcomes for beneficiaries, campaigning offers organisations the prospect of increased membership, higher public awareness of specific issues, a heightened public profile and the chance to increase funding opportunities.

THE RIGHT AND DUTY TO CAMPAIGN

Voluntary sector campaigning has been responsible for many of the rights and entitlements that we now take for granted. Organisations in the sector are uniquely placed to represent the needs and aspirations of their beneficiaries and members: it is the business of those who make up such organisations to have an intimate knowledge of all the issues relevant to the causes and people they represent.

Not only do voluntary organisations have the right to campaign, they also have a duty to communicate the needs and wishes of their beneficiaries and members to those in a position to make decisions and provide solutions.

Where a voluntary organisation works to address a specific need or cause, there is no clear dividing line between its role as service provider and its role as public advocate of that need or cause. Campaigning is thus an integral part of the core activity of voluntary organisations. The growth of service provision as a function of the voluntary sector has led to a similar growth in campaigning activities.

Campaigning has achieved significant improvements in the quality of life for many people, raised levels of environmental protection and standards in the care of animals. What's more it has also contributed to a fundamental change in the way civic life is conducted at both the local and the national level. Campaigning has led to the growth of new forms of consultation with statutory authorities and user groups and has become a focus for representing local interests. It has also become a means for citizens to exert a meaningful influence over national decisions and policy making and has gone some way toward re-establishing a sense of civil responsibility and community. At the same time, more people, dissatisfied with political parties and existing opportunities for involvement in civic life, have signed up as members of charities and pressure groups. Many of the larger voluntary organisations now have memberships greater than those of political parties.

These changes have happened against a background of increased state control over local finance and decreased opportunities for people to influence local or national service delivery as previously accountable government agencies have been replaced with 'next steps' agencies and quangos. An active and involved citizenry has never been more needed and involvement in pressure groups, as a means of expressing social concern, has been noted by political commentators as a growing trend.

However, campaigning has also come under increased scrutiny from the public and the media. There is growing unease about the role of parliamentary lobbying. Many people believe that the practice exerts undue influence and distorts the democratic process. While most attention has been focused on the activities of commercial lobbyists, the voluntary sector cannot presume that its own standards and practices will not also come under greater scrutiny. In such an environment, it is particularly important for the sector to be able to show that its practices are above reproach and that its campaigning activities are pursued with the same professionalism as any other area of activity. In the case of charities, the board of trustees plays a significant part in this.

Campaign Tactics: Insiders Vs Outsiders

Traditionally, the most common way to distinguish between campaigning organisations was to classify them either as Sectional Interest Groups, such as trade unions, business associations or professional bodies, and Cause Groups representing a public interest, such as charities and single-issue lobby groups. However, both the behaviour of organisations and the complexity of the environment in which they now operate have broken down such simple distinctions. Interest groups now define their agenda more broadly – supporting, for example, environmental projects and the employment rights of disabled people – while cause groups protect and nurture their organisations, as well as seeking to enhance their beneficiaries' interests.

A more useful way of understanding campaigning organisations is to look at the strategies and tactics they use to achieve their ends and the public positioning they need to adopt. Academics and campaigners have found it useful to divide campaigning organisations or particular campaigns into two general types: 'insider groups' and 'outsider groups' (Grant, 1995: 20).

Insider groups are those who seek legitimacy and acknowledgement from those they hope to influence with the target of the campaign fro example members, government ministers or the public. Outsider organisations are those who either do not wish to achieve such status because they are ideologically opposed to the existing system, or do not have the resources or the sophistication to achieve it. The insider/outsider distinction is useful in analysing where organisations or campaigns sit within the spectrum of possible campaign strategies and activities.

Grant (1995:20) identifies the positions an organisation or campaign group can occupy in relation to decision makers (see Figure 1). This classification is not static and organisations can move to some extent between different approaches as a campaign develops. It may even be possible for the positioning of an organisation to change depending on the nature of the campaign. It is important to recognise that charities occupy slightly different terrain from other campaign groups because of the restrictions imposed by the Charity Commission guidelines governing campaigning by charities. It is unlikely that pressure groups which are charities, and which wish to retain their charitable status, would take up the position of an ideological outsider group.

Figure 1: Typology of campaigning relationships

Type of relationship	Characterised by
Insider groups	
1. 'Prisoner' groups	• Find it difficult to break away from government or decision-making body because of their dependence upon funding or because of a statutory role in relation to the sponsoring body.
2. 'Low profile' groups	• Working mainly behind the scenes in specialist areas.
3. 'High profile' groups	• Insider groups that reinforce their position with government, statutory authorities or business by careful use of the media and public opinion.
Outsider groups	
4. Potential insider groups	• Organisations currently outside the main policy circles which may have the capacity, by representing a coherent interest and having the resources, to win insider status.
5. Outsider groups	• Those lacking the sophistication to win insider status or who tactically decide to use the outsider route after all insider routes fail.
6. Ideological outsider groups	• Those groups opposed to the existing system and/or those which think that change cannot be achieved through the existing system.

(Source: Grant, 1995:20)

The power of this approach is that it focuses attention on how campaign groups actually behave and what strategies they employ to achieve their objectives. *The Good Campaigns Guide* focuses on the methods used by groups that seek to alter behaviour, attitudes or policy, rather than focusing on the organisational distinctions between different kinds of groups. The guide also highlights some of the particular factors that distinguish charity campaigning from the activities of other voluntary organisations.

THE IMPORTANCE OF VOLUNTARY SECTOR CAMPAIGNING

The size of the voluntary sector is significant and growing. Kendall and Knapp (1996), using what they term a 'narrow' definition of the sector, estimate that there are between 200,000 and 240,000 voluntary organisations in the UK. The Charity Commission states in its annual report for 1994 that it expects registered charities to increase by 8,000 a year for the foreseeable future. Many of these organisations will, at some time, become involved in representing their interests to decision makers and the public.

Campaigning has grown as public confidence in the government's ability to provide solutions to problems has declined; with this has come the need for voluntary organisations to develop a political dimension to their work, whether in direct representation of their clients or as a response to the complex organisational environment in which they operate. The voluntary sector accounts for a significant proportion of the pressure-group activity that goes on every day of the week, from parliamentary lobbying to local campaigning for better services. Campaigning by charities and voluntary organisations now makes up part of the fabric of political life at national and local level.

A survey of campaigns in the voluntary sector conducted for NCVO found that, of 191 members, 77 per cent saw campaigning as integral to their other activities (Healey, 1991). Campaigning by voluntary organisations has grown significantly in recent years and this growth is reflected in the sheer profusion of campaigns. These have included campaigns calling for a reduction in the age of consent for homosexual men, the introduction of new rights for disabled people, the prevention of dumping of industrial waste at sea and the establishment of measures to protect the countryside, habitats of rare species and rights of way for walkers.

The growth in the number and scope of campaigns conducted by the voluntary sector has been accompanied by an increase in the complexity of the political environment in which the sector operates. Recent developments included:

- a decline in the state provision of services to vulnerable groups and a consequent growth in voluntary sector activity;
- the emergence of competition between voluntary groups in the sector as an alternative means of ensuring the equitable distribution of social resources;
- a change of emphasis towards advocacy and campaigning;
- the success of high-profile campaigns leading others to see this as a route to protect or enhance their position;

- competition between groups for supporters and volunteers;
- an increase in the environmental concerns of large sections of the population;
- a decrease in the confidence of business and the public in the ability of government to get legislation right;
- a breakdown of trust in government to provide solutions to individual or community problems;
- an increase in the need for government to consult with those dealing with problems on the ground due to a lack of first-hand knowledge about client groups or issues.

The need to adapt to this changing environment has led campaigners to becoming more sophisticated in their strategies and techniques and has increased the need for trustees to have a good understanding of the processes of campaigning. *The Good Campaigns Guide* is designed to help trustees and staff understand these processes and work together to develop campaigning strategies and standards which are appropriate for their organisations.

CHARITY CAMPAIGNING

The legal framework in which charities operate imposes restrictions not shared by other voluntary and trade-sector pressure groups. While most of the principles outlined in this book are generally applicable to groups of any size, from small community charities to large national bodies, particular attention must be paid to the legal context in which charity campaigning takes place. Principally, charities are accountable to their beneficiaries, as represented by the board of trustees, and are covered by the Charity Commission's guidelines on political activities. These key distinctions between charities and corporate and sectional-interest groups are rooted in charity law and this is dealt with in more detail in Section 5.

IN CONCLUSION

The growing influence of pressure groups brings new responsibilities. Public opinion has the potential to limit both the role and effectiveness of such groups and, if the voluntary sector loses the support of the public, it will also lose its power. It needs to demonstrate that the backing, including money, it receives from the public is used effectively in the pursuit of the causes it espouses.

The Good Campaigns Guide sets out a framework for sharing some of the best practice that exists for managing and developing successful campaigns in order to help the sector address the challenges it will face as campaigning develops.

Part 1.
Planning Campaigns

I.

Pre-Campaign Planning

THINKING IT THROUGH

Many groups are drawn into campaigns without considering how they are going to achieve their aims. The selection of strategy, method and tactics is crucial to the success of a campaign. The choices an organisation has will depend upon its resources and its overall standing with the public, its customers, statutory agencies, the government and the media. This, in turn, rests on an organisation being seen as the legitimate representative of the client group or issue it claims as the target of its campaign.

To develop a strategy, organisations need to be clear about what they are trying to achieve, to make an analysis of the environment in which they are operating, to decide on clear goals and to identify ways of achieving them by:

- understanding how change happens;
- making an analysis of the political situation and the issue;
- identifying the organisation's strengths and weaknesses;
- deciding on clear goals for the campaign;
- agreeing the methods and tactics to achieve those goals;
- monitoring the impact the campaign is having;
- evaluating what happened;
- using this information in the next campaign.

MAKING CHANGE HAPPEN

Understanding how political change happens will increase the likelihood of a successful campaign. While there are some factors that relate to successful campaigns in general, other factors are very specific to individual projects. It is possible to identify some of the key elements of successful campaigns.

The model below was developed from an academic study of pressure groups and politics (Grant, 1995) and an analysis of successful campaigns examined for the Guide.

Issues Central to an Organisation's Ability to Pursue a Successful Campaign

Organisational Issues
- the stability of the organisation, group or alliance;
- the capacity to take decisions and resolve conflicts within the group or campaign;
- the financial resources to sustain the campaign, and staffing and experience available to the campaign;
- the availability of different strategies and the effectiveness of the one chosen;
- the ability to apply sanctions to the target of the campaign;
- the characteristics of the potential membership being organised or represented (some groups may be far better positioned, because of their membership, to progress a campaign);
- the ability to be seen as the legitimate representative of the issue or group by the target of a campaign;
- the ability to attract members and mobilise them to support the campaign objectives;
- the ability to construct and maintain alliances;
- the level of support from the board of trustees and senior management.

External Issues
- the extent to which public opinion is favourable to the issue being promoted;
- the public profile and reputation of the organisation promoting the issue;
- the group's reputation with the media;
- the attitude of the party in office towards the issue being promoted;
- the economic circumstances, especially in relation to public expenditure, if this is relevant to the campaign;
- the credibility and power of the target of the campaign;
- the time-frame of the decision-making process;
- the existence of sponsorship or support by a government department.

All the above elements could be used as a means of examining how an organisation is positioned to achieve change.

Campaigning will always be opportunistic and luck often plays a part in politics and campaigning. However, those with the most well—developed plans are best placed to take advantage of opportunities that could not have been predicted. How to plan and implement a campaign will depend on the size and nature of the activity. Not all of the factors outlined above will apply to every campaign. What is given here is a simple model of strategic planning that is intended to prompt questions and ideas to help in devising any kind of campaign.

Campaigns go through a number of different stages in planning and implementation. Figure 2 represents these stages that need to be taken into account in planning and implementing a campaign.

CREATING A STRATEGIC FRAMEWORK

The development of a strategic analysis and planning framework is a means of ensuring that the factors outlined in Figure 3 are considered. Once it has been established that an issue is central to an organisation, it is important that, firstly, campaign objectives and secondly, success criteria are developed. The strategic analysis should help in defining achievable objectives for the campaign. From this, it is then possible to define what actions will be most appropriate to achieve those objectives. It is important that the chosen criteria against which the relative merits and the success of any campaign are to be measured reflect the strategic issues relevant for the organisation.

BEFORE YOU BEGIN

The factors that provide the key to successful campaigning differ with each campaign and it is helpful to establish a process whereby these can be listed and evaluated. The essential point is to concentrate only on those factors which will have a significant impact on achieving the campaign objectives. Below is a list of the kinds of questions that organisations need to ask before embarking on any substantial campaign. By working through the questions, a planned approach to a campaign can be achieved. In the next section, some of the issues relating to these questions are explored using case studies of some of the organisations surveyed for this book (see Appendix 2).

Figure 2	
Key Questions	**Factors to be considered**
What is the importance of the issue for the organisation?	How does the issue compare with others that the organisation is dealing with? What is the impact on the client group relative to other issues?
How is the organisation	Assessing the credibility of the organisation in relation to this issue with key audiences, i.e. the public, press, key professional

positioned on the issue?	bodies, other opinion formers. These audiences must be clearly identified and can be plotted on a chart to clarify the organisation's position.
Is it possible to identify the key levers of change and the appropriate decision makers?	Ensuring that the target of the campaign is really the most appropriate. Assessing what connections the organisation has with those who make the decisions or put pressure on the decision makers. It is not always necessary to promote legislation or a change in policy to remedy a situation. It could be that the issue is one of broad attitude change which would imply a different kind of campaign. It may be one that could be resolved through legal action: judicial review of local authority decisions can be a powerful weapon in areas of service provision and benefits.
How does the issue compare with other issues currently under consideration?	Comparing the costs of the campaign and its potential impact with other projects. Draw up a list of other potential projects and establish criteria for evaluating the proposed campaign against these. For example, the RSPCA deals with up to 200 campaigns in any one year. It is essential the organisation has a clear process for establishing which campaigns will be given priority.
How strong is the evidence?	Is there enough evidence to establish the issue? This could include research evidence from the provision of a service or commissioned or in-house research.
What can be done?	Producing clear objectives for the campaign. Constructing a sensitivity analysis of how achievable these are and how long they might take. SWOT and PEST analyses can be used to Inform these discussions (see Appendix 2). Major factors will be the cost of the proposal and the scale of change that would be required, e.g. do the aims require primary or secondary legislation or an administrative change? Primary legislation is far more difficult to achieve than an administrative adjustment.
Is campaigning the only way this change could be achieved?	Asking whether the aims could be better achieved by early negotiation or by alternative means such as service provision. Assessing other remedies, i.e. the local government ombudsman or consumer representation.
What is the potential cost of the campaign?	Assessing the cost of the proposals demonstrates that they are credible and that they have been well thought through. It also restricts the opportunities for opponents to claim unrealistic

	costs for the proposals or dismiss them without coming up with alternative costs. The benefits, or potential savings of the proposals, should also be costed.
What is the potential importance of the issue?	Assessing public concern on the issue and the organisation's ability to mobilise its members or client group. For example, the Ramblers' Association knew that rights to access was a key concern for its members and that it had public sympathy while WWF conducted a poll of potential members to establish their level of concern about the environment.
What is the state of expert opinion on the issue?	Establishing the state of expert opinion and assessing whether this is of value to the cause or provides ammunition for opponents. Assessing the need for and ways of acquiring technical advice, for example, on the law, a procedure or an international agreement.
What intelligence is available on other relevant issues that may be emerging from government business?	Ensuring that intelligence is gathered about the issue and the decision makers' likely reaction to demands. Do the demands fit in with central or local government or business policy or seek to overturn existing policy? How firmly are those policies held and how central are they to those being lobbied? What other interests might support the case or be opposed to it? What other policies are anticipated and how important are these compared with the issue under consideration? What other factors affect the target of the campaign? Is there a national or local election coming up? Are there prominent backbenchers that would support the cause? How much would the demands cost to implement? Is the timing for the campaign going to mesh with the decision-making process? What are the most significant economic and social factors, relevant legislation, statutory responsibilities and general social trends affecting this issue?
Has the organisation the capability to deliver the campaign?	Evaluating what level of resources the organisation can commit to the campaign. Deciding upon and costing campaign tactics. Assessing whether the campaign relies on the mobilisation of the members and whether the organisation has the means to do this. If the organisation does not have the internal resources, can these be commissioned from other agencies, i.e. political consultancies?

What is the potential for making alliances with other organisations and will there be opposition?	Assessing the potential for forming alliances with organisations that share a similar view and evaluating potential problems in constructing such alliances. Asking whether the alliance has enough common ground and understanding and whether the allies have a similar organisational background as well as the ability to work together successfully. Assessing whether there are significant groups in the sector which will oppose the campaign and whether anything can be done to address or neutralise the concerns raised.

The campaign staged by the RSPCA over the Wild Mammals Protection Bill illustrates some of the issues connected with taking a strategic approach to campaigning.

Case Study
1. The Wild Mammals Protection Bill

The Royal Society for the Prevention of Cruelty to Animals (RSPCA) was faced with a clear strategic decision about compromising a long term aim to ensure that an achievable objective could be delivered. Crucial in this was the relationship with the trustees and the way in which they worked through the strategic issues together to reach an outcome that was acceptable for the organisation. The RSPCA also had to attempt to neutralise the opposition of other powerful groups and ensure that it could count on the support of potential allies.

THE CAMPAIGN
The RSPCA sought to close a loophole in the law which gave protection from cruelty to domestic animals but not to wild ones. The organisation had been campaigning for this as part of a wider move to ban blood sports and had already been involved with two previous bills. These had not succeeded because the hunting lobby had enough support in both houses of Parliament to ensure that the measures failed.

To link the demand for protection for wild mammals to a call for a ban on hunting as part of the same bill would ultimately cause the campaign to fail. It was therefore decided that a single-issue campaign should be run with the aim of securing legal protection for wild mammals. The campaign was aimed primarily at MPs, although public awareness advertising, media work and the RSPCA supporters were also used as part of the overall campaign.

Senior managers and trustees needed to agree with the change of position. Decisions about campaign priorities caused debate within the organisation. The RSPCA has for a long time opposed blood sports and some people within the organisation were worried that a 'watered down' campaign would damage the organisation's position. By having a clear evaluation of the chances of success plus a detailed campaign plan, staff were able to secure early organisational support for the campaign. Although originally sceptical, the trustees agreed that a successful campaign would be better than an heroic failure. The argument for limited change was strengthened by recent RSPCA failure to win a number of high—profile cases involving cruelty to wild animals.

The Society put a number of options to Alan Meale MP, who had come second in the private members' ballot, and he agreed to propose The Wild Mammals Protection Bill, which had been the RSPCA's favoured option.

ALLIES AND OPPOSITION

Many MPs were already allies of the RSPCA. However, the power of the hunting lobby, which remains particularly potent in Parliament, was still a serious concern to it. A decision was taken early to try to enlist the support of the British Field Sports Society (BFSS), a pro-hunting organisation traditionally opposed to the RSPCA but which was identified as an organisation without whose support no bill of this kind could get through.

As well as behind-the-scenes meetings and contacts, an exhibition was organised at the House of Commons to explain the purpose of the campaign and give information about the proposed bill to MPs and other interested groups. This generated interest among the key target group of MPs and allowed a public exhibition of co-operation with the BFSS in advance of a second reading debate on the bill, helping to ensure that opposition to the bill from that quarter was limited. The dialogue that this exhibition opened up is regarded by the RSPCA to be one of the most important parts of the campaign for the effect it had not only on MPs but in neutralising opposition.

Supporters were also drawn from the voluntary sector from animal welfare groups. Seventy organisations signed up to the aims of the campaign, allowing the campaign to claim broad support among key constituencies. Similarly, the government were approached at a relatively early stage and, although a certain amount of negotiating had to be done, it also agreed not to obstruct the bill. The government recognised the levels of public support the bill had and, in addition, did not feel it represented a major threat to hunting,

which at that time was an important internal issue for the
Conservative party.

Pressure was put on MPs via a national letter-writing campaign
generated by the RSPCA. The organisation asked its supporters to
write to their MPs and local papers about the issue and encouraged
them to come to the House of Commons for the second reading of the
bill. In line with its general practice, the RSPCA rejected the
possibility of employing other tactics, such as a mass lobby of
Parliament or demonstrations, as such actions would not fit the image
of the organisation and could harm the campaign.

PUBLICITY

A major broadsheet advertising campaign was launched, with the dual
aim of raising public awareness and inspiring further letters to MPs.
The advertising was hard hitting (following the RSPCA house style)
but based on factual cases which could stand up to public scrutiny.

A key feature of the campaign was the use of animal case studies.
'Kelvin' the hedgehog was an effective case which captured the public
imagination. He had been sprayed with red paint and his bristles had
fallen out, but the perpetrators of this cruelty could not be
prosecuted. Photos of Kelvin were used, and the case had a powerful
effect on public opinion and the media, turning the issue into one
which affected 'real' animals and was therefore of genuine concern.
The case had a happy ending in that Kelvin's photo was used by the
Conservative MP Michael Fabricant in the eventual debate as an
example of the kind of animals the bill sought to protect. Not long
after the bill was passed, the hedgehog's missing bristles grew back!

Because the campaign had successfully united MPs and the public,
its passage through Parliament went smoothly. The second reading,
committee stage, report stage and third reading were all taken in one
sitting; an exceptional parliamentary procedure.

By being clear about the objectives of the campaign and matching
these to the political environment in which the organisation was
operating, the RSPCA were able to achieve a substantial change in
legislation.

2.

Issues in Campaigning

IS YOUR ORGANISATION CREDIBLE?

It is important for organisations to ensure that they are well positioned to take up an issue. The case an organisation presents will in part depend upon the way it is viewed by those it is trying to influence. This, in turn, will depend upon factors like the size of the client base or interest group it represents, the level of expertise it brings to a situation, the quality of the specialist knowledge available to it and the extent to which this is unique to the organisation. Whether the organisation is seen as being pre-eminent in its field and how far it is believed to be reflecting a genuine or widely held viewpoint that has, or could, enlist public support and sympathy, will be other deciding factors in an organisation's presentation of a cause.

The issue of power also comes into this equation. The credibility of many large multi-national groups is already well established, at least in part because of the position they occupy within the economy as employers and providers to the local community and national economy. However, reputation and positioning are important and, as such organisations are often vulnerable to negative publicity, large corporations spend considerable time and effort ensuring that their credibility with the public and government is protected and enhanced. The ways in which large multi-national groups establish and protect their credibility will, of course, differ from those adopted by smaller charitable organisations. The key point is that the organisation needs to assess its credibility and potential vulnerability to criticism before embarking upon high profile, public campaigning.

TRUSTING THE TRUSTEES

Within the charities the board of trustees plays a key role in the governance of organisations. The more resources organisations invest in campaigning, the more trustees need to know about what constitutes good practice. Trustees need to know what questions to ask of campaigners and to understand how they go about their business. Communication between campaigners and trustees can be difficult because the board, especially in larger organisations, is often removed from day-to-day activities. This can be compounded by the complexity of legislation and the mystique that surrounds the workings of Parliament and politics, especially for trustees unfamiliar with the political system. Ensuring that campaigners and trustees can work together in partnership is a prerequisite for enabling organisations to take a strategic approach towards campaigning. It also allows for the views of board members to influence campaigning activity.

> As Hudson (1995: 283) notes in his work on voluntary sector management:
> *Boards of campaigning organisations play an important role in achieving the right balance of campaign flair and sound management. Although board members will be passionately dedicated to the causes, they need to be able to stand back from the details of individual campaigns and play a more strategic role.*

IDENTIFYING THE LEVERS OF CHANGE

It is important for organisations to ensure that they have correctly identified the root causes of the problem they seek to address and have isolated the key points at which to apply pressure. It is pointless to mount a campaign based on political pressure if the government department, business or agency which has the power to affect a change has not been identified. Campaigners need to distinguish between political, administrative and legal solutions to problems; those failing to identify the most appropriate route will be wasting their time. These areas may overlap, and their boundaries are not always easy to identify. For example what appears to be an administrative blockage may actually be a policy problem which requires the intervention of policy makers or politicians. If campaigners do not identify the levers of change correctly, they will not only waste resources but they will also irritate those they seek to influence by focusing on institutions that cannot take the decisions required.

The task of the campaigner has become much more difficult with the proliferation of 'next steps' agencies and the contracting out of many national and local authority services. Voluntary organisations must closely examine the operating environment and status of the body they are trying to influence. Many areas that were previously in the control of the executive now come under the auspices of bodies that are commercial enterprises in law and hedged round with confidentiality clauses that prevent public scrutiny. Whatever the status of the decision-making body, campaigners need to identify clearly who has the power within that organisation to take decisions relevant to the issue at hand. Only when this has been done can the channels of influence and pressure points of a decision-making body be mapped out.

TARGETING THE CAMPAIGN

Having identified the key decision makers and agencies empowered to achieve change, the next important step is to target campaigns for maximum impact. Clearly, how this is done will depend to some extent on the aim of each campaign. A survey conducted in 1992 suggests that voluntary organisations rate targets for parliamentary campaigns in the order of importance illustrated in Figure 3, where one is high and nine is low.

Figure 3

Group	Rating
Civil servants	1
Ministers	2
The media	3
Parliament	4
Particular sector of public opinion	5
Public opinion in general	6
Other pressure groups	7
Political parties	8
One political party	9

(Source: Baggot, 1992)

Civil servants and ministers are the judged the most effective targets for organisations wishing to make advances in legislation or dispute government initiatives. The remaining subjects on the target list are less effective but may be used to put pressure upon the first two. The list also reflects the priority order in which many campaigners tend to work through the various layers of the political structure, assuming they already have some insider status in relation to the policy community they are working with and that the issue is already established.

While all of the campaigns studied for this book shared a similar focus on the key targets we found that the particular context could often make a difference to the sequence in which these targets were approached. However, campaigners should not make the mistake of thinking that they must always start at the highest level possible within the political structure. Many issues can be usefully raised by non-ministerial contacts before they have to be referred to ministers for decisions, as the civil service and statutory agencies work by delegating to the lowest level necessary to deal with a decision. The priority of the targets will often depend on whether the contact in question is the prime target, i.e. the minister or civil servant who can take the decision, or whether, like a backbench MP or the media, they function only as a conduit to put pressure on those making the decisions.

Different ratings could be developed for campaigns targeted at local authority agencies or companies. The following table, indicating a possible ranking for campaigns targeted at local authority decision makers (where one is high and seven is low), has been developed from the analysis of a number of campaigns focusing on local authorities.

Figure 4

Group	Rating
Local authority officers (directors of a service)	1
Council committee chairs	2
Local media	3
Local MP	4
Local authority officer (senior post)	5
Individual councillors on committees	6
Individual councillors	7

USING POLITICAL CONSULTANTS

Many campaigning groups have used political consultants with success. Before employing consultants there needs to be a clear brief developed for the agency to ensure that the organisation is certain about what it expects and why an agency is being used. Political consultants have been most effectively utilised in cases where the organisation lacks in house expertise or appropriate contacts for short term projects, and when economies of scale make outside agencies particularly effective at tasks such as parliamentary monitoring and intelligence which would otherwise take a disproportionate amount of time and expense for individual organisations.

When working with a consultant (or consulting agency) voluntary organisations must:

- have a clear understanding of the advantages of using the consultancy over internal staff
- develop a detailed brief for the agency which should be discussed and agreed with them
- create a budget for the project to be shared with the agency, there should be a clear mechanism for agreeing any changes to this
- make sure that the consultant you select has expertise in the areas you need. Ask to see a list of the other clients that the agency represents this should help to give an indication of where its expertise and focus lies. Different consultants and agencies have different strengths. Some concentrate on the financial services sector or public sector others have strengths in public relations or links to advertising agencies. Some agencies are also

parliamentary agents and have particular legal expertise in drafting legislation which is especially useful if lobbying on private members legislation or other private bills

- obtain a number of bids from competing consultancies
- ensure that someone in the organisation has the responsibility for managing the contact with the agency and insist on regular briefing or updates on work in progress.

The use of political consultants does have to be handled sensitively. The public positioning of the organisation can be questioned if it is to closely associated with a commercial lobbying agency because of the associations this has with trying to procure undue influence through professional advisors. It might also be assumed that the organisation was not confident in the moral authority of its position to present the case itself. For these reasons it is not advisable to let an agency or consultant handle the direct contacts with the target of the campaign. Secondly, where there are professional campaign staff within the organisation they need to be involved in the relationship with the agency or consultant so that there is proper co-ordination of activity and that the internal staff do not feel supplanted by the use of outside help.

It is almost never advisable to use consultant's staff to represent or accompany the organisation in a meeting with Ministers or officials. This sends a clear message that the organisation is not confident of its case and is trying to purchase influence via the agency. Use agencies for their expertise or ability to monitor the environment.

Though expensive consultants can be very cost effective for groups of all sizes if used well. It is also the case that they sometimes offer different rates to charities and campaign groups either because of the profile of the issue(and hence commercial benefit to the agency if they succeed) or because of the value of having a broad range of clients on their books.

Families Need Fathers used a political consultancy to help them respond to the government's white paper which first floated the idea of the child support agency. This white paper was clearly going to be critical for the future of their members and with only one full time staff member they did not have the time or internal expertise to produce the paper in time. The consultant's paper was then used to structure the campaign to considerable effect. This was an effective use of an agency where the organisation had limited resources. It should not just be presumed that it is only the largest campaigning organisations that can make effective use of political consultancies.

TASK PLANNING

When the strategic analysis of the proposed campaign has been completed and its objectives have been defined, a plan of specific actions or tasks may be drawn up. The main elements of a campaign plan could be summarised as follows:

Figure 5

Campaign plan stages	Key points	Notes
• **Identify key tactics in line with strategy and objectives**	• What tactics would be appropriate for the organisation and the campaign objectives? • Identify staff resources and timing. Liaise with others affected. • Are the objectives measurable and clear? They should be: specific, measurable, achievable, realistic, timed and money costed.	• Produce timetabled plan. • Ensure that campaign actions are clearly identified on the plan. • Ensure the plan is developed and shared with relevant departments, stakeholders, and members.
• **Identify messages of the campaign and what audiences they are targeted at**	• Campaign materials developed. Checked for appropriate tone and style. • Details on audiences and channels of communication collated.	• Check printing schedules and costing. • Ensure any advertising agencies, etc., are aware of the timetable and internal guidelines.
	• Key targets entered on mailing lists and monitoring system for responses established. • Timings for press work and mailings agreed.	
• **Plan print schedule**	• Timings for printed material and design agreed	• Ensure that print and design timetables fit with campaign timetable and designers are aware of any special requirements, i.e. accessibility guidelines for printed material.
• **Plan campaign actions**	• Campaign actions established and arranged. Supporters briefed, if they	• Ensure that supporters are mailed in sufficient time to be able to take the actions

Campaign plan stages	Key points	Notes
	are involved (see action plan, Appendix 1).	required. Make sure a full briefing and background to the action is included.
• **Establishing legitimacy**	• Campaign actions and materials checked against legal requirements and existing guidelines (see Part 4).	• Ensure that all campaign materials are checked for libel, etc. and that all planned actions are within the law. Ensure all actions and materials of charity campaigns follow Charity Commission guidelines.
• **Monitoring**	• Set up procedures to monitor the campaign.	• Isolate what elements of progress can be measured and identify key milestones for the campaign.

THE USE OF PLANNING TOOLS

There are a number of planning tools that can assist in the development of the strategy and the plan of action. The main ones are detailed in Appendix 1 with some suggestions about how these might best be used.

CONTINGENCY PLANNING

It is advisable, if the size of organisation allows it, to leave spare capacity of resources and time deliberately on the assumption that things may go wrong or that the focus of the campaign may need to be altered.

Many of the steps outlined above could be gone through within the course of a meeting depending on the scope of the issue, the resources and size of the organisation.

The following case study shows how some of the important factors examined above were drawn together in a campaign. The Carers National Association (CNA) were keen to establish the legal right for carers to have an assessment made of their service provision needs. The organisation targeted backbenchers and opposition parties in an attempt to bring pressure to bear on the decision makers. As in so many situations, the breakthrough came when civil servants and ministers indicated that they were not hostile to the aims of the private member's bill.

Case Study
II. Carers National Association

The NHS and Community Care Act 1990, which came into force in 1993, included the right for disabled people to have an assessment made of their needs for social service provision, but there was no such right ensured for carers. The aim of the campaign was to achieve, for carers, the legal right to such an assessment via a private member's bill. The secondary intention was to achieve a legal commitment to provide services and resources to carers as a result of assessment.

The Carers' (Recognition and Services) Act 1995 started life as a simple two-clause bill. It placed a duty on local authorities to carry out assessments of carers and to provide them with services.

A formal plan was drawn up for the campaign. It was assumed that there was no immediate prospect of a change in the law. Civil servants, the media and the general public were all considered important targets since all had the power to put pressure on the government. Communications were co-ordinated and conducted from the national head office of CNA and involved the members in letter-writing campaigns and making constituency contacts.

The Labour Party was specifically targeted to get its support for the bill. The party accepted the principle of CNA's case in a document it published late in 1994. At the same time, channels of communication were being opened up with civil servants and government. These contacts were then followed up with a delegation of MPs (all carers themselves) to the then Secretary of State for Health, Virginia Bottomley JP MP, who had been briefed by CNA. The aim of the meeting was to present evidence that the new system was not working and see how far the government might be prepared to move towards CNA's position.

There are two inherent problems to overcome with a private member's bill. First, finding an MP high enough up the ballot to have a reasonable chance of the bill being discussed. Secondly, there is a restriction imposed on any private member's measure which means the government cannot be committed to providing the resources to implement the proposal.

Malcolm Wicks MP, a supporter of CNA, agreed to table a backbench bill on the issue when he came tenth in the private members' ballot. This changed the pace of the campaign and meant that CNA had to plan a much more high profile campaign if it was to gain public support and pressure MPs and the government into supporting the bill.

CNA decided to broaden the campaign to reach the public and the press in advance of the second reading debate in March 1994. This effectively left three months for a plan to be put in place and support for the measure canvassed amongst key audiences and allies. While this timetable gave the campaign a clear goal, it also produced potential hazards. Because the bill was only tenth in line there may not have been time to debate it in parliament, so all the work was jeopardised by the pressure of the parliamentary timetable. On the other hand the campaign was helped by the amount of consensus around the bill.

As part of the campaign, a meeting was secured with the minister responsible for community care, John Bowis MP. At this meeting CNA established that the government were not wholly opposed to the bill, but, with adjustments, would be prepared to pass it. As a result of the Bowis meeting it was felt that, if CNA put enough pressure on the government, the bill might get through. CNA began to encourage its members to write to their MPs and organised a lobby of Parliament. This took the form of a tea party for carers which got substantial coverage and raised the issue clearly in the minds of MPs.

An important alliance was formed with other supporters of the bill to publish separate but related research on the carers issue. The organisation arranged a joint press conference with Scope and the British Medical Association to present supporting research, all of which generated further media coverage and added to the momentum of the campaign.

The campaign ended with the passing of the bill in July 1995. The final stages were not entirely straightforward, however: although the government had accepted the principle behind the bill, CNA needed to adapt its demands and, to an extent, compromise in order to ensure that the bill would get through its all—important second reading. Crucial in this negotiating process was the use of lawyers by CNA in its discussions with ministers and civil servants, to ensure that whatever negotiating was done, the substance of the bill would not change too dramatically.

A key change was the dropping of the demand for adequate resources to support the assessment of need. This demand was opposed by the government on cost grounds. A pragmatic decision was taken to accept the government's view once the principal argument for a legal right to assessment had been accepted. CNA reasoned that arguments for resources could continue in the future but if the organisation had tried to insist on extra resources at this stage, the whole effort could have failed.

Co-operation with the government made the third reading of the bill run more smoothly than is usual. The committee stage took place on the floor of the House of Commons, thus ensuring that the bill did not run out of time. Additional pressure on the government ensured that the provisions applied to all carers, not just to those over 18 years of age as the government had originally wanted. It was important even after the successful passage of the bill through the House of Commons that the campaign continued in order to ensure a safe passage through the House of Lords.

External factors played a part in the success of the bill — principally the ongoing debate about community care and the potential damage it could cause. The government were also vulnerable on disability issues having blocked the passage of the civil rights private member's bill earlier in the year.

3.

POWER, DECISION MAKING AND SANCTIONS

The American political writers Bachrach and Baratz (1966) noted that power has two faces. It is necessary to look not only at which issues are favoured by government or decision makers but why some issues are either absent from the political agenda or are dropped from it. This second area is much more difficult to assess. The reasons why certain issues never make their way into policy are often unstated or unclear. It is in this area where the second face of power operates.

To make strategic analyses of what options are open to an organisation and what is possible, the second face of power must be taken into account. The sanctions that an organisation may have explicitly tried to apply to government and decision makers — and the effect this threat may have had on the final decision — will not always be clear. Pressure groups often operate around the margins of this second area by trying to stop government or decision makers from passing legislation or creating policies adverse to the interests of their client groups before they reach the public political agenda. The fear of the reaction a lobby group might have may, in some instances, be enough to prevent decision makers putting particular measures before the public.

There are also the more obvious sanctions that campaigning organisations will seek to apply through a campaign. The principal sanction is clearly public pressure but there are a number of other means to exert influence. It can be helpful to think of campaigning as a progression through a number of stages from negotiation to public campaigning. Campaigns may start on different points of the continuum depending on the situation but many will move from one sanction to another or employ a combination of approaches. Sometimes legal remedies will offer a different route by which to apply pressure.

Figure 6 Campaign Styles

Style	Negotiation	Public pressure	Public action	Legal remedy
Sanctions	• Using expert opinion to challenge the target • non-co-operation in the development of proposals • non-public pressure; letters to ministers, chief executives, etc.	• Public pressure from client group sensitive to public opinion • Pressure from members on publicly sensitive issue • Slowing up of legislative or policy proposals	• Demonstrations • Boycotts of goods and services • Stunts • Occupations • Vigils	• Judicial review • Individual court cases • Class actions • Tribunal cases • Product liability cases

Campaigns may begin with a non-public attempt to create change. An organisation may chose to advance the issue via public pressure, if this fails, advancing to direct public action if there is no resolution. Campaigns can start by employing both private and public pressure but the tone and style of the public pressure may change depending on the nature of the response from the target of the campaign. It is important to ensure that options for resolution are explored before mounting a public campaign. Public pressure puts the target into a corner from which he or she cannot publicly retreat; it may prove counter productive in cases where negotiation is possible.

Clearly there are times when the combination of pressure-group politics and public opinion can set the national agenda for government or, at least, to shape the existing agenda. This is often due not just to the campaign itself but also to the extent to which pressure groups are able to capitalise on a swing in public opinion. Public opinion remains the pressure group's principal sanction on central and local government and business.

This aspect of campaigning is dealt with in more detail in Part 2 which discusses styles of campaign communication.

FORMAL AND INFORMAL SYSTEMS OF INFORMATION

Both the formal and informal pressures on policy making must be taken into account. Many campaigners, while attempting to alter the formal policy-making process, ignore informal routes and, by doing so, either miss opportunities or fail to identify all the elements which may influence a decision. A good campaign will take all these routes of influence into account in its planning and execution.

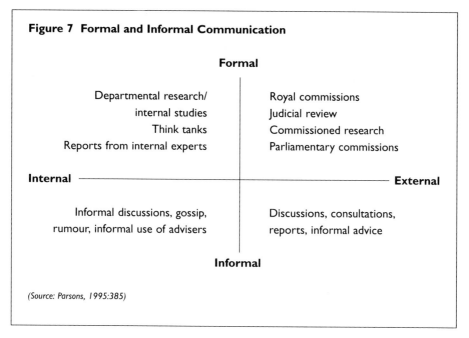

Figure 7 Formal and Informal Communication

Formal

Departmental research/	Royal commissions
internal studies	Judicial review
Think tanks	Commissioned research
Reports from internal experts	Parliamentary commissions

Internal ——————————————————————— External

| Informal discussions, gossip, | Discussions, consultations, |
| rumour, informal use of advisers | reports, informal advice |

Informal

(Source: Parsons, 1995:385)

In addition, there are a number of different channels of communication available to campaigners which can be used as paths to achieve campaign objectives.

Voting and Campaigning

Many organisations hope that the pressure they exert on particular issues may be reflected at the ballot box. Research shows that people make up their minds on how they will vote in relation to a complex set of beliefs and influences. It is very unlikely that many voters base the way they vote on a single issue, except perhaps in the case of certain emotive issues such as abortion or membership of European Union. Therefore, apart from concerns that the Charity Commission may have about attempts to influence the way people vote, such tactics will often be misdirected and will only have a slight impact on how people vote. This is why the attempts of some organisations to construct voting alliances for disadvantaged groups have failed and will continue to do so. Local elections may reflect more local concern with service issues (especially such issues as hospital closures) but, even here, there is no simple correlation between voting patterns and single-issue campaigns.

UNDERSTANDING THE WAY VOTERS VOTE

The voting framework below is a simplified version of an analysis developed by Coxall and Robins (1994). It looks at the determinants of voting preference and helps explain why the hope that an allegiance to single-issue politics or causes will translate into pressure at the ballot box is too simplistic. There are a wide variety of influences on how people vote. Undoubtedly pressure groups play an important role in influencing voting behaviour and allegiance to a single issue may indeed partly determine voting on related issues. Yet the overall picture is one in which a number of other determinants on how people vote come into play. This is especially true where campaigners have sought to isolate certain interest groups, such as benefit claimants, and sought to construct political allegiances towards a set of policies on this basis.

Figure 8 Determinants of Voting Preference

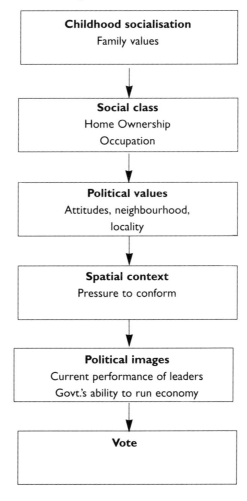

Using Opinion Polls to Focus a Campaign

Opinion polling can be a useful way of gauging the support for a case and helping to focus a campaign. However, given the costs, which are high even for established national charities, campaigners need to be extremely clear about what constitutes an appropriate use of opinion polls in targeting or evaluating campaigns.

For example, polling Members of Parliament could provide:

- a clear picture of the views held by MPs on a particular issue at a specific time;
- the ability to target a campaign in the light of knowledge about how MPs perceive the issue;
- the possibility of tracking changes in perception in relation to the campaign over time. For example, the gay rights organisation Stonewall evaluated the changing perceptions of MPs towards the age of homosexual consent. A poll in 1991 showed that only 11 per cent of MPs favoured 16 years as the age of consent for gay men, but, after a concerted campaign on the issue, this figure rose to almost 50 per cent by 1994;
- the possibility of gauging the effectiveness of a campaign message.

Opinion poll results can also provide campaigners with valuable material around which to base press releases, interviews and so on, in support of their campaigns which, in turn, can also help to shift the public or MPs' perceptions in favour of the cause.

MPs are obviously not the only group it may be useful to poll. Many campaign organisations poll their members and the public on issues of concern to establish what views are held on particular issues or what impact a campaign is having on public perception.

Beware the pitfalls of polling

There are a number of considerations that need to be taken into account to ensure polling gives useable results:

- Campaigners must be clear about what it is they are monitoring. Opinion polls are better at measuring reactions to and views on topical issues than addressing the sets of deeply held values that may go towards making up those views. Focus groups or one-to-one interviews may be a better means of assessing such underlying values.
- It does not necessarily follow that, because MPs express a level of support for a cause, they will actually vote accordingly. Furthermore, political parties will often apply the 'whip' to members who may, therefore, vote contrary to their particular views on an issue.

- Opinion polls are not good at gauging the strength with which a view is held and this may also lead to discrepancies between a poll result and actual behaviour. This can often be partly compensated for by comparing the poll data with other information, for example, with feedback from supporters or contact with MPs.
- It is possible for respondents to misrepresent their opinions or intentions, or to be misleading in their answers. A famous example of the latter was the discrepancy between stated voting intentions and actual voting patterns at the general election in 1992. The opinion polls overstated the level of Labour support because Conservative voters were less willing to reveal to pollsters their party allegiance. A similar effect can also apply to polling on other issues where respondents are unwilling to reveal opposition to a cause perceived to be popular or where they deceive themselves about the behaviour they would exhibit in a given situation.
- An opinion poll is only as good as the questions it asks. The questions must be as specific as possible and, while polling agencies will be able to frame questions in an appropriate way, they have only a limited knowledge of what campaigners are trying to achieve. Most opinion polls on public services, for example, will show that the electorate are in favour of increased public expenditure in these areas. However, this apparent level of support drops when the means of paying for these services, such as raising income tax by specified amounts, is taken into account.
- Opinion polls are a useful tool for campaigners but can be misleading if read outside the context of other evidence that is available.

During a 1994 campaign to ban the transportation of live animals, the RSPCA ran advertisements in the press giving a telephone helpline number. In two-and-a-half days, the number of calls in favour of the organisation's position was 70,924 with only 2,384 calls against. The poll provided a clear measure of public feeling on the issue and the RSPCA was able to use the results to bolster its case for change (NCVO News, December 1994/January 1995: 12).

Case Study
III Using opinion polls

During a campaign for civil rights legislation for people with disabilities, Scope, formerly The Spastics Society, wished to find out the existing level of support for the principle of legislation to introduce a right of non-discrimination for disabled people. With this information Scope hoped not only to gauge the level of support for such a measure but to assess how far this would lead MPs to support a private member's bill. The survey would also allow comparison with an earlier study to gauge how far the level of public support had increased or decreased over the period of the campaign. One of a number of secondary issues that also needed to be assessed was how far the current campaign had alienated MPs and public opinion. Scope commissioned two surveys, one of MPs' views and one of public opinion.

The survey of MPs asked a number of questions about how far members would support civil rights legislation, what the key issues within the legislation would be and what their perceptions of the cost of the legislation were. The survey showed growing support for the measure on a cross-party basis but not at a level that was necessary to carry the House of Commons in a vote over a private member's measure.

Shortly after the survey, the government brought forward its own bill in response to a broad-based campaign around the issue, but it was of a much more limited nature. The information in Scope's survey was then used to target parliamentary activity on the government's bill at those areas where there appeared to be a high level of support. This targeting did not always translate into defeats for the government, as MPs cannot always vote with their conscience, but it had proved to be a fairly reliable indicator of the areas where most success could be gained. Scope continued to support the campaign for more comprehensive legislation, as this was a long-term organisational priority, and used the survey results to predict the chances of such a measure having success within the term of that Parliament.

The survey of MPs and the public also showed that Scope's campaign had not alienated supporters, as some press reports had claimed. Support among the public had increased by four per cent during the period between the two polls, which confirmed that the high profile the campaign was attempting to achieve was not too strident and had not put off potential supporters.

Because the survey was conducted by an independent research company, it was difficult for the government to ignore the results.

FORMING USEFUL ALLIANCES

The ability to form and maintain alliances is one of the keys to successful campaigning. Many voluntary campaigns benefit greatly from being conducted in alliance. Joining forces with sympathetic partner organisations can often help campaigners in the presentation of a case as well as lending it credibility. As with alliances of trade associations the main aims of such arrangements are to speak out with a common voice on a particular issue and to add weight to a campaign. There are many areas of life which are affected by political activity but few in which there is only one interested party and, given the power of government and business, an alliance of voluntary sector agencies will have a far stronger voice than any individual organisation.

Clearly, there is nothing more damaging to a campaign than a disagreement between significant organisations in the voluntary sector. Decision makers targeted by campaigners will happily exploit any divergence of views within the sector, often giving this as reason enough for not changing their stance.

However, working in alliances can present difficulties and there are a number of major issues that need to be addressed. Potential partners need to be identified and approached; other groups with an interest in the issue should also be consulted and kept informed of progress to ensure that, if they do not sign up to the alliance, they will at least not take up a stance of active opposition.

Campaigning in alliances is time consuming and requires careful preparatory discussion and planning so that potential difficulties are anticipated and a clear basis for co-operation is established between the organisations involved. There are a number of key issues which should be addressed jointly by all member organisations in the initial stages of forming an alliance:

NEGOTIATION
Procedures must be agreed for making decisions on tactics and positioning. In alliances with many partners it is not always possible for all members to meet on a regular basis and mechanisms for delegating tasks to — and receiving progress reports from — small groups or individuals should be devised.

IDENTIFYING RESOURCES
Member organisations will bring different skills and levels of finance to an alliance. These resources should be identified and agreement reached on what each member will contribute.

POSITIONING THE CAMPAIGN
The tone and style of campaign should be agreed and should accord with the profile of all member organisations.

Agreement should be reached on which members will co-ordinate the press and publicity work and who should act as spokesperson. Alliances can frequently benefit from nominating a lead organisation which, because of its position or size, is best placed to carry out the media work for a campaign.

However, the strength of an alliance lies in its ability to represent a broad range of interests. It is also important that alliance members do not feel that any single organisation is benefiting disproportionately from the publicity and an effort should be made to give all members equal media exposure.

INTERNAL COMMUNICATIONS
Working in alliances can lead to confusion between different departments within member organisations. It is important for campaigners to maintain clear links with their own press departments to ensure that they are aware of the media

issues. Local groups must also be kept fully informed so that the best use can be made of local alliances and local support.

Joint Publications

Producing publications can be a time-consuming and costly enterprise and alliance members should take particular care to avoid duplication.

Joint statements, reports and other publications must be agreed by all member organisations, at least in relation to policy conclusions or any demands that flow from this.

Alliances and the Law

Member organisations need to devise mechanisms for ensuring that the activities of the alliance and its other members do not breach the law (see Part 4). Member organisations risk being held jointly liable, for example, for campaign messages that are considered libellous or appear to support a specific political party during the course of an election, even if they are issued by another member organisation. Charities must pay particularly attention to the requirements of charity law and the Charity Commission guidelines (Charity Commission, CC9).

There are a number of well-established principles for the formation of campaigning alliances:

- coalitions or alliances need a sound basis of mutual interest over a particular concern;
- the alliance must have a clearly defined aim that all members can ascribe to;
- the contributions of members should be negotiated and clearly defined before any campaign work begins;
- there should be an early opportunity to discuss openly the expectations and aims of the partners;
- there should be room for differences — as long as these are clearly acknowledged and do not contradict the aims of the campaign;
- the alliance should not be used as a vehicle for an individual organisation to promote itself at the expense of the other partners or the issue;
- there should be no free-loaders and recognition should be given to the different resources that member organisations may be capable of bringing to the campaign and the varying strengths they may have;
- where possible, an explicit budget should be agreed between the different organisations to finance all campaign activities.

Many organisations are fearful that campaigning in alliances will lead to a lack of control over the content and aims of a campaign and, further, that the carefully nurtured public positioning of an organisation will be swallowed by the common identity of a coalition. Furthermore, campaigners attempting to achieve change through alliances may find that they must tailor their objectives to fit in with those of their campaign partners. This can mean that campaigners must demand less or, more typically, as the needs of the new allies are accommodated, the demands of a campaign must be made more wide reaching and less concise. Campaigners must strive to maintain a balance between building an alliance and achieving the campaign ends or they face the risk of failure on both counts. This has become particularly important because, due to the overlapping interests that now exist between organisations, campaigners rarely carry out projects entirely on their own.

Case Study
IV Roads to Ruin

The campaign outlined here is very different to others given as case studies in the guide since it was aimed at changing government policy and spending decisions. The aims of the campaign were reflected in the methods used and in the need for a broad alliance of different groups. One of the keys to the campaign's eventual success was the effective use of the alliances together with the mobilisation of public opinion. This example illustrates the importance of having a clearly defined case and being able to present this via the appropriate channels. The ability to co-ordinate what was an extensive lobby was also a key factor in that it prevented the campaign losing focus and degenerating into a series of local actions with no national focus. It also serves to highlight the importance of ministers: getting agreement for the campaign objectives from the existing minister to ensure that his successor followed a similar policy was a key step.

BACKGROUND
The Roads to Ruin campaign was co-ordinated by Transport 2000, a lobby group set up to work on transport issues. The campaign started as a result of the government's 1989 announcement of a £300 million road programme in the form of the Roads to Prosperity document. Transport 2000 (T2000) wanted these plans scrapped.

The main target audiences were the Treasury (because of concerns over the cost of the programme), the media and other politicians. The public were also targeted, not so much in an attempt to change their attitudes to using cars, but in an effort to educate them about what the environmental and economic impact of the road programme would be.

T2000 met with a range of other interested groups and produced a response to the paper called Roads to Ruin. Following this the groups decided to continue meeting and to co-ordinate information, forming the Transport Round Table. This was a broad coalition of environmentalists and transport users whose key aim was to shift the political agenda and promote a change in political culture. Internally, the campaign sought to ensure that there was much better co-ordination between local anti-road groups than there had been in the 1970s during the last round of major road building.

Transport Round Table co-ordinated the campaign and, for the purposes of this particular activity, the other groups within the Round Table acted as the members. Local government also began to support the campaign, as authorities realised that the roads being built in their areas would entail significant extra costs for them.

The main opposition was the road lobby, which consisted of car retailers and manufacturers, the freight industry, the construction industry, the AA and the RAC. As a counter to these last two groups, who claimed they represented the wishes of 'ordinary road users', T2000 and others set up the Environmental Transport Association, which provided the same services as the AA and RAC, but took an opposite view on road building. Although the road lobby had once been a formidable opponent, it was slow to respond to the concerted campaign of the Round Table and rapidly discovered that it no longer carried the weight in the media, or in Parliament, that it had once enjoyed on this issue.

THE CAMPAIGN

The Department of Transport which was proposing the programme was a target for the campaign. Because it was often impossible to get answers from the Department of Transport, the media began to use T2000 as its main source of information on the roads programme which helped to establish the credibility of the campaign.

Many Conservative MPs began to take the issue seriously, partly because the M25 road building/expansion was a high-profile issue, giving their sympathy to the campaign. The appeal to MPs was made more effective by the fact that the local groups were part of a national campaign and that this was not a simple constituency matter but part of a wider political issue. The local groups were well served by the campaign and consequently felt part of a wider movement which helped to keep their enthusiasm high.

While T2000 and others did a lot of lobbying, independent research and media work, other groups, particularly grass roots local groups, were taking direct action, achieving substantial press and television coverage which kept the issue on the agenda.

Co-ordination of information was the key to ensuring that messages did not become confused: far from fearing the negative consequences of direct action for the campaign, T2000 were able to show that the action was locally based and legitimate. Since road planning procedures left so little room for public input and dissent.

The other key element was to show the media, the public (and the Treasury) how costly road building was and why the plans would not lead to prosperity but to economic ruin.

Key developments were the watershed public protests at the M11, Twyford Down and Newbury. It became clear that, after these protests, road building in this country would not be planned or conducted in the same way again. The fact that T2000, via the Round Table, had been doing the background work meant that the organisation could keep the behind-the-scenes discussions going as the government became increasingly embarrassed by the level of public anger about these and other road building/expansion schemes.

Other important developments were the meetings that began to take place between MPs from constituencies affected by the M25 and their colleagues in other parts of the country who were experiencing similar problems. Again, the strength of the campaign and the way it had brought together local issues into a coherent, national, political debate meant that these meetings became significant in changing the political culture.

Furthermore, the environmental, anti-road arguments that the campaign was putting forward made it difficult for the government to justify such a massive road building programme. This was because the UK had signed up to the pledge on sustainable development at the UN's Rio environmental summit.

Finally, Steven Norris MP, when he was Transport Minister, was very impressed when the campaign took him to York to see the city's traffic-free city centre. As a consequence he decided that there were many alternatives to road expansion. He was influential in persuading his successor, Brian Mawhinney MP, that this was the case. The ongoing meetings of the Round Table, and the mix of direct action and behind-the-scenes work meant that the campaign was flexible enough to react to, and benefit from, these key developments.

4.

Membership and Client Groups

THE IMPORTANCE OF INVOLVEMENT

The recruitment and retention of members is important for campaigning organisations to ensure both financial support for campaigning and to add weight to the representations of a group. This is true for large international organisations and small community associations alike. For many groups, the members' time and energy will be their main resource; campaigns will benefit if actions are targeted in a way which enables the members to participate and which plays to their strengths. The Carers National Association urged its members to write to MPs with their own experiences. The organisation also held a tea party at the House of Commons, which allowed some of the campaigners to meet with the relevant minister in a non-confrontational setting (see Case Study 2). The campaign group, Stonewall, organised a vigil outside the House of Commons to put pressure on MPs during the passage of a bill to lower the age of consent for homosexual men. Both these campaigns promoted involvement by the members in actions that were appropriate in style for those organisations. The needs of the members, as 'customers' of the campaigns they are taking part in, should be considered. The style and content of the material produced, the actions requested of members, the amount of time it will take them to complete those actions and the support materials or training that they may need are all important considerations which have to be addressed.

Of the organisations surveyed for this guide, The Ramblers' Association, Amnesty International and the RSPB all produced campaign supporter packs to help their local groups campaign. The information supplied in these packs ranges from general advice on how to plan a campaign using standard planning techniques through to more detailed instructions for planning specific campaign actions. Also included are house style rules for press releases and suggestions on how to use the evidence supplied with the packs. Many organisations now invest large amounts of resources to ensure that their members are skilled campaigners and that they are effective in pursuing the aims of the campaign set by the national organisation within the boundaries agreed by the parent body. The actions members undertake will clearly depend upon the level of development, the type of organisation, and the nature of the campaign.

Amnesty International have a strong international network of campaigners who can be mobilised at short notice to take part in concerted campaign actions co-ordinated with other approaches such as mass media coverage. Case Study V illustrates how, when there is a clear objective and a pressing timescale, planning and action can be accomplished very quickly. What is important to remember, however, is that Amnesty International is able to respond in this way because of the planning and effort that had gone into the construction of an international network of supporters, organisational credibility and policy development in the past.

Case Study
V Amnesty International

Amnesty International has campaigned consistently against the application of the death penalty under any circumstances. Thus, when in 1995 the Nigerian Government sentenced the prominent environmental activist Ken Saro Wiwa and nine other Nigerian dissidents to death, Amnesty International mounted an urgent campaign of action. Time was of the essence since the Nigerian Government had set a period of only ten days between sentencing and execution.

As Campaigns Co-ordinator Rob Beasley explained, there was very little time for campaign planning. 'We had to move very rapidly to get a public profile for the issue'. This urgency was in part balanced by the clarity of the issue: to save Ken Saro Wiwa and the others from execution. The plan therefore focused on getting maximum media impact for the campaign in the shortest time possible. The main aim was to get the public to put pressure on the Nigerian Government, partly through their own appeals and partly via their appeals to the UK Government. The campaign also targeted the oil company Shell both because it was the largest corporation with an interest in the issue and because Shell's operations in the area had been the object of the dissidents' protest. As well as creating a lot of media activity the UK section of Amnesty International urged its local members to join a concerted letter-writing campaign through its urgent action network.

The style of the campaign was determined by the gravity of issue: its straightforward approach reflected the imminent loss of life and the perceived injustice of the process. The main campaign tactics were the use of the media and the placing of emotive hard hitting advertisements in the press. These high-profile activities were combined with concerted action by the members writing letters and holding vigils.

Because of the level of media coverage, there was a great deal of optimism that the campaign would be successful. However, it was difficult to estimate the impact that this was having on the Nigerian Government who remained silent throughout.

Tragically the campaign ended with the execution of Ken Saro Wiwa and eight other political prisoners. The campaigners were taken by surprise as, right to the last moment, they had hoped that the Nigerian Government would grant a stay of execution.

Amnesty International has continued to use the same media techniques and inventive stunts to gain coverage. A large picture of Ken Saro Wiwa was projected onto the wall of the Nigerian High Commission in London a year after his death. This image was captured and reproduced by the news media and therefore seen by millions of people. While the campaign to save the lives of the dissidents was unsuccessful, the international coverage gained pushed the issue of the use of the death penalty up the political agenda. This has created a situation in Nigeria where any further such decisions by the Government are likely to receive considerable publicity and generate international concern.

Throughout, the campaign received massive international coverage because of the prominence of the central person and the emotive appeal of the issue. However, according to Beasley, Amnesty International has since had many internal discussions about the 'style of some of the material used'. Although it is important to generate an emotional reaction in the general public, campaigners should maintain a balance, especially in an area as complex as human rights, and the propagation of images presenting oppressed people as passive victims should be avoided.

Organisations that represent and benefit from the involvement of user groups are clearly in a different situation than those whose members are mainly recruited via direct mail campaigns. Organisations that can mobilise user groups have especially strong credibility with decision makers as they have the authority to be truly representative. Government and other decision makers are likely to see such organisations as being able to speak for their client group, negotiate on their behalf and give an assurance that the members will abide by the outcome of such negotiations. If they are not able to deliver such agreements, their credibility with decision makers will be damaged.

Memberships or client groups have influence within the political system according to the extent that they are seen as representing a popular or deserving cause — and the extent to which they can apply sanctions against the target of the campaign. Threats to publicly embarrass the target or to make something a national issue at election time are just two of the sanctions that groups can apply. However, some of the tactics of mass campaigning and pressure-group politics have to be used with care. Most MPs, local councillors and European politicians have become hardened to the mass letter-writing and petition-signing campaigns as their post-bags have become full. Campaigns that find ways of reflecting concern that bring home the personal costs to constituents are likely to have more chance of success.

TIMING

Many of the case studies completed for The Good Campaigns Guide stress the importance of timing for the success of a campaign. The shorter a campaign is, the fewer possibilities are open to it and the chances of success are reduced accordingly. Once proposals are in the public realm, there is less chance of achieving a change, not least because of the reluctance of those in power to be seen to give way under pressure. Clearly, once proposals are made public, they will already have gone through a number of discussion processes and those involved are likely to be committed to their plans. In addition, at this stage, there is simply less time available in which to mobilise opinion against the proposals and to find alternatives.

The ability to take action early is vital for campaigning organisations, particularly when they are responding to publicly-made proposals. For campaigners to be able to do this, organisations must have good contacts with relevant officials at national and local level and must put in place effective monitoring systems. The press and reports of government, local authority and committee proceedings are all good sources of information which it is important to monitor regularly.

5.

THINK NATIONALLY ACT LOCALLY

The effectiveness of campaigning on a local level depends on the same principles as national campaigning. Groups need to be well organised, have a clear understanding of the issue and be able to back up their claims with well—presented evidence. They need to be able to show decision makers that their group has the support of the community and be able to mobilise support for their position among elected representatives. Ideally, campaigning groups will have constructive relationships with local officials or business representatives.

The Charity Commission have issued separate guidelines for local community charities. These restate the principles applied in CC9 (see Part 4) to the circumstances of local bodies (Charity Commission 1997(a)). Community groups and local campaigning organisations will not have the same level of resources and time as larger organisations and this should be taken into account in the planning and management of campaigns.

Local organisations tend to get involved in two different types of campaign; local action as part of a national campaign and local action responding to a local problem.

LOCAL CAMPAIGNING IN ASSOCIATION WITH A NATIONAL BODY

When a group takes action as part of a national campaign, many factors will already have been decided by the parent organisation. The main planning issue will be to ensure that the actions and tactics of the campaign are suitable for the local circumstances and relate to the group's needs. For example, if a national campaign selects local authority social services departments as a target and the overall campaign is very strident in tone, a group which has a good relationship with its particular local authority will need to alter the tone of the campaign to preserve good relations.

While local variations will always have an impact on the nature of a campaign, national and local organisations should ensure that there is adequate consultation between them to avoid unnecessary confusion, muddled campaign objectives or inappropriate tactics. The parent body must develop campaign proposals in consultation with the members or local groups, implementing feedback mechanisms, some of which are outlined in Chapter 4. Conversely, local groups and members must check with national parent bodies before taking local actions to establish whether the parent body has a specific policy relating to that issue or recommends a particular approach. In addition campaigners for registered charities need to be aware of the expectations of the Charity Commission with regard to local campaigning and the activities of local bodies of national organisations (see Part Four, Keep it Legal!).

The principle focus for much of the campaigning work of the Ramblers' Association is via its 400-strong, local-group network which it actively encourages to take up campaigning. The Association gives information and support to local group campaigns which include lobbying local authorities to open up rights of way and taking action against farmers who plant crops on footpaths. The head office will only take up local campaigns at the request of local groups and prefers to encourage these groups to do their own campaigning with the support from the centre. Groups may publish records on access to rights of way in an attempt to highlight which authorities are good at protecting footpaths and which are not — embarrassing the bad ones into taking action. Groups are also encouraged to write letters to local councillors and the press in order to influence local opinion about the need for more footpaths.

Although the Association is able to produce Ordnance Survey maps in court as legal documents to enforce rights of way, this is only used as a last resort. Fortunately authorities usually take action as a result of local-group campaigns. Thus, it is particularly important for the Ramblers' Association national body to provide clear guidance to local groups on how to campaign. The Association also makes extensive use of its local groups as a source of field information and feedback.

Some organisations seek to balance the requirements of the national body with initiatives by local groups and members by developing very clear campaigning practices, specifying the types of actions members may undertake. A high level of control is needed in a situation where inappropriate actions by the members could lead to damaging consequences for the campaign or for the individuals involved, or where a particular campaigning practice has proved so successful that it would be wasteful not to repeat it.

Amnesty International has a very clear and structured set of campaign formats and so similar patterns are followed by all Amnesty International campaigns, irrespective of the urgency of the case in question. Members receive a timetable, a clear set of instructions and a format to follow. This process has been established because of the potential danger to prisoners of conscience should an action go wrong plus the need to ensure a constant and speedy response from the members.

In contrast, there are some campaigns where groups on the ground must be allowed to tailor their activities to respond to local circumstances. In these cases, the parent organisation must develop a "hands off" management approach — while still monitoring, informing and supporting local activity.

National organisations can work very effectively with local branches or members in pursuit of national objectives though local action. Typical types of activity are: the recruitment of campaigners at regional level, the contacting of MPs to support particular issues through local contacts and the highlighting of national issues through regional examples. Oxfam has established a system designed to raise the profile of issues at the local level whereby contacts with MPs and MEPs are recorded and passed back to the Oxfam campaigns team. Clear guidance both on charity law and Oxfam's aims and objectives is given to local groups to ensure that they stay within the boundaries defined by the organisation. Support materials include simple forms for recording contacts made and identifying the targets for contact (see Figure below).

TARGETED RECRUITMENT

MPs and MEPs can be categorised at the regional level according to their importance and past support for Oxfam. It is suggested that regions should prioritise recruitment of constituency contacts in the constituencies of supportive and important MPs/MEPs. The following categorisation should be used by regional offices:

Figure 9: Oxfam regional recruitment plans

		Potential influence			
support for Oxfam	High	1	2	3	4
	Medium	2	3	4	5
	Low	3	4	5	6

If an MP/MEP's position is plotted on this grid it is envisaged that the closer s/he is to the top left-hand corner of the grid (e.g. the lower the number in the grid), the higher the priority for recruitment.

Key requirements for local campaigning

- clear guidelines covering campaign style and tone are drawn up by the national centre for the use of local groups;

- appropriate methods for discussing and communicating campaign priorities between local groups and the national centre are settled. Ideally, there is a clear constitutional link between the members and the local bodies;
- appropriate training and support is made available for local groups to achieve any campaign objectives set by the national organisation;
- local groups are made aware of the Charity Commission's guidelines, where relevant, and the law in general relating to campaign activities;
- a system is set up to deal with any complaints about the activities of local groups and to react quickly and effectively if the campaign has overstepped legal or internal guidelines. Depending on its constitution, a national organisation could be held responsible for the actions of local groups;
- an evaluation mechanism is set up so that local groups can give the national body feedback on how useful campaign materials and support have been.

CAMPAIGNING BY LOCAL ORGANISATIONS

The activities of local, independent voluntary organisations still need to adhere to the basic principles of good campaigning. However, the resources available to such groups will vary and this will have an effect on the planning and implementation of campaigns. Further, most local campaigns differ from national campaigns in that they often originate from a spontaneous reaction on the part of individuals affected by a particular event. This produces a very different dynamic to that of a well-planned national project developed by an officially constituted body. Local campaigns are frequently run by people who have never worked together before and who may come from disparate backgrounds and have different skills. This can be a great strength for a group but only if the energy is directed in ways which make best use of the group's resources. The major resource that most community groups have, of course, is the people who support the campaign.

PLANNING LOCAL-GROUP CAMPAIGNS

Whatever the size of the group, the time available for campaigning and the nature of the issue, it is still essential to go through the major stages of planning.

THE ISSUE
The issue may be simple — lack of adequate access to a local school, closure of an accident and emergency facility at the local hospital, blocking of a local right of way — but it still needs to be stated clearly and the consequences for those affected spelled out.

RESEARCH

Where possible, evidence of an issues' impact must be given. This may appear simple — for example: a stipulated number of people are to have a particular service withdrawn — but the key message of the campaign must focus on the impact that such a withdrawal of service will have on the individuals concerned. Existing research from local authorities and other such sources can be used.

THE ALTERNATIVES

Campaigns should be constructive, indicating, for example, why the planned changes are not going to achieve the results claimed and proposing an alternative course of action.

IDENTIFYING THE CORRECT TARGET

Campaigners must identify those who can take the necessary decisions and target the campaign accordingly. This is not always a simple task; for example there are still many areas where there are three tiers of local government and, if the campaign is addressing an employment issue, this may be covered by a Training and Enterprise Council or the local Office of the Department of Employment. For each campaign, the organisation must take into account the local decision-making structure and the relationships between the various administrative bodies involved.

SEEKING ALLIES

Valuable support for campaigns can often be found within the local community or from other national bodies and, on occasion, one local agency can be enlisted to support a campaign aimed at another. Professional associations, local businesses and civic dignitaries will often offer their support and local politicians and MPs should be informed, when appropriate.

TONE AND STYLE OF CAMPAIGN

For a local group to present its views with a consistent voice to the public and the press, its members must come to an agreement regarding the public profile of the campaign. Also, groups need to decide when to raise the profile of a campaign from one of behind-the-scenes negotiation to a more vociferous public protest.

THE CAMPAIGN PLAN

With limited resources it is crucial that effort and money are not wasted. Local groups need to draw up a clear action plan based on a realistic assessment of how much time people can really give. A 'skills audit' of all the members of a group should be conducted, to ensure that the abilities of those involved are put to good use: members should also be asked to list all local contacts they may have. The campaign should be reviewed and adjustments made to the plan as the situation develops and the timescales set should be realistic.

EVALUATING THE CAMPAIGN

Each campaign should be evaluated and a record kept of which actions failed and which ones were successful. Supporters should be thanked and contact lists kept.

Many national campaigns have started as local campaigns initiated by one or two charismatic individuals. These have resulted, for example, from legal challenges to the decisions of local authorities, often conducted with the support of a national body, or from the activities of a local group creating a groundswell of public opinion that is echoed in other parts of the country. In one instance a campaign to stop local authorities charging for home-care services, started by a single carer in Kent and another group in Liverpool mushroomed into a national campaign which drew support from national organisations and mounted a successful lobby of Parliament.

The following case study illustrates the importance of focusing on the key issue of a campaign and ensuring that all the available local support is mobilised and that the correct targets are identified and approached in an effective way.

Case study
VI. Local issue local action

A group of disabled children attending a specialist unit attached to a mainstream school were denied visiting physiotherapy support during school hours. Such support was essential to ensure that the children remained mobile and could participate fully in the curriculum. Many of the children had a statement of special education need which specified that they required this support and which, in theory, should have ensured its provision.

A group of parents approached the health authority only to be told that the current arrangements whereby the authority provided an occasional visit to advise parents or offered support over the phone was adequate for their needs. Not satisfied with this the parents formed a group to campaign for the introduction of a regular visiting physiotherapy service.

In an effort to raise the profile and establish the gravity of the issue the parents started with a letter-writing campaign contacting members of the health authority, the local physiotherapists and their MP. A meeting with the local MP followed after which he forwarded many of the letters to the Secretary of State for Wales, the local Director for Education and the General Manager of the Health Authority. Despite these efforts, the health authority continued to maintain that the current arrangements were adequate.

At this point, the parents decided to set up an action committee in order to give the campaign more profile and weight. The local MP was invited to be the chair of the group and the parents approached the Chartered Institute of Physiotherapy hoping to gain their backing. The Institute offered its support to the case that physiotherapy is best provided for in the situation most suited to the children and that visits to hospital were rarely appropriate even if they did maximise the use of the physiotherapists' time. It was also pointed out that the pupils where having to miss whole days of schooling to attended the local physiotherapy department.

The campaigners contacted the health authority again but this time got the children affected to write their own letters detailing the effects that the lack of therapy was having on them. One pupil wrote,

'I desperately need physiotherapy because I am starting to seize up. When I was in primary school, I regularly received physio, but when I left it was like as if I was cured. Before I didn't feel so bad but now I can feel myself seizing up.'

The combination of the children's letters, the professional opinion of the Institute of Physiotherapy and the high profile the campaign achieved through the involvement of the local MP seems to have had its effect on the authority. The campaign group received a letter from the health authority outlining its intention to provide physiotherapy from the start of the new financial year.

In Conclusion

A strategic and planned approach to campaigning helps to ensure that the objectives of a campaign are achieved.

Campaigning is a complex activity which can be organised and planned in the same way as other areas of business and charitable activity but which has particular sensitivities that make prediction of the outcome complex. This is more, not less, of a reason to ensure that proper plans are in place when undertaking campaign activity.

Part 2.

Attracting Publicity and Raising Public Awareness

6.

A BALANCED VIEW

'When I see a lurid headline I say fine…but when I look at the small print I want to see the argument.'

(Peter Snow, Broadcaster, Institute of Charity Fundraising Managers Conference, 1991)

Many campaigning organisations are extremely well supported and some, such as the Royal Society for the Protection of Birds, have memberships that are bigger than those of political parties. The challenge for every organisation is to promote its cause clearly and convincingly to the relevant constituency and to a general public whose attention is being competed for by many other issues.

One of the major goals of any campaigning organisation is to raise public awareness of its existence and its aims. Some organisations put their resources into creating a heightened awareness period of perhaps a week or month to raise public awareness of a specific issue, such as the Royal National Institute for the Blind's 'Eye Health Campaign'. Many organisations also seek to achieve general or corporate awareness to keep their name and activities in the public eye. This may be achieved by using specific 'hooks' such as newspaper advertisements for donations, press coverage, corporate advertising and other marketing activity. All these activities raise awareness of the organisation and provide credibility that supports and underpins other campaigning activities.

During the expansion of campaigning there has also been a revolution in the methods and techniques used to convey messages about an issue or cause. Campaigns themselves have grown in complexity; their messages and their means of communication are more sophisticated than ever before. Some marketing techniques, such as high-profile advertising and direct mail activities, are now a standard part of campaigning. The list below gives a number of common forms of campaign communication:

- publications/leaflets/brochures

- videos
- broadcasting
- advertising
- direct mail
- syndicated tapes
- exhibitions
- drama
- floats
- events and promotional stunts
- petitions
- the Internet

The potential reach of such techniques and the influence they have over the general public has made pressure-group campaigning more visible and brought a much larger audience into contact with its views. However, some politicians have become concerned that the public is often manipulated by pressure groups who do not really command the level of support suggested by their profile.

The powerful imagery and emotive appeal that typifies many pressure-group campaigns has also raised questions about the way people and animals are depicted in the pursuit of campaign objectives. Strident campaigning has brought campaign groups into conflict with media regulators on a number of occasions. This has caused heartfelt debates within campaign organisations about the balance between emotive appeal and the need to explain issues in a tone that wins the long-term support of the public and press, rather than achieving only short-term publicity.

The relationship pressure groups have with the media is also being questioned, especially by broadcasters and journalists. The media's close relationship to pressure groups that are able to provide journalists with hard-hitting stories has led to accusations that the reporting of pressure-group claims is not subject to the same level of critical scrutiny reserved for political parties. The media is the quickest route to immediate publicity for an issue but it serves neither pressure groups nor the media when the two are viewed as being too cosily hand-in-glove.

Campaigning has also seen the adoption of many of the techniques of direct marketing. This is not altogether surprising: For many campaign groups, whose aims are to change opinion and gather support on a large scale, the methods of mass communication prove both practical and useful.

Many appeals now work to achieve a high media profile while carrying out a campaign of direct marketing. This has led to concerns that issues are being packaged and marketed like soap powders. However, given the size of the memberships of many of the larger campaigning organisations, it is difficult to see how else they could recruit and communicate with their members. Campaigners and fundraisers have to balance the need to achieve maximum impact for a campaign with the duty to abide by the values of their organisation.

This can prove difficult when the message needed to maximise income is not necessarily the same as that which will achieve particular campaigning objectives. The needs of campaigning, corporate positioning and publicity often become blurred because of these competing pressures. Difficult choices have to be made in the way organisations seek to use the media and position themselves in the public eye, particularly because the treatment of an organisation or campaign by the media may not always accord with what was intended.

Responsible use of the media and public pressure is an accepted part of the process of influencing government and business. As long as it is carried out in a way that makes dialogue possible it provides important extra buttressing for discussions that go on inside Whitehall or the board room. Given that there is a competition for attention between various causes, a level of publicity and evidence of public concern is going to be a crucial part of any attempt to keep an issue on the agenda with ministers, civil servants and the public. This raises a number of complex issues for campaigners to consider.

POSITIONING THE ISSUE

The presentation of a campaign message can make a huge difference to the outcome of a campaign and to the way an organisation is perceived. This is explored below in relation to a Greenpeace campaign on industrial waste which involved the organisation in staging an occupation of an oil rig in the North Sea.

The strategy of Greenpeace in occupying the oil rig Brent Spar – and then providing its own video footage of the occupation to the news media – was spectacularly successful in generating coverage of a campaign about the disposal of industrial waste. The campaign was confrontational and strident in tone. This was in keeping with the campaigning style Greenpeace members and the public had come to expect. However, the way the organisation positioned the debate had consequences for how the campaign progressed and how Greenpeace was perceived.

Case Study
VII. Greenpeace and the Brent Spar campaign

Brent Spar was a redundant oil platform which the oil company Shell wanted to dispose of in the North Sea. Consequently, Brent Spar was chosen by Greenpeace as a symbolic focus and was occupied by activists in an attempt to stop its disposal and highlight the issue. The campaign was about industrial responsibility and the use of the sea as a dumping ground. During the course of the campaign, this focus was lost: the disposal of Brent Spar and the question of how much toxic material was actually on the rig became the major.

Greenpeace had developed a campaign plan that was based on raising public awareness, getting the public involved with the issues, and using public concern to influence the UK Government. Getting news coverage was the organisation's main tactic. Greenpeace succeeded by using dramatic television footage of direct action on and around the platform. Video news releases generated significant media coverage on national news bulletins. Greenpeace realised that the media coverage was more pro-government than it would have wanted, but felt that it had got its messages across. Media coverage of Chancellor Kohl of Germany raising the issue with Prime Minister John Major at a European summit meeting helped increase the profile of the campaign.

Putting pressure on Shell was seen by Greenpeace as another means of achieving the primary campaign aim of a change in government policy on industrial disposal. Consequently, the oil company also became a target and Greenpeace groups were encouraged to organise local activities such as picketing Shell petrol stations. Although it was ultimately up to the government to resolve the situation by prohibiting dumping, Shell was in a position to change the site for disposal of the Brent Spar and so became the focus of much activity.

Style of campaign
Although Greenpeace tried to keep the campaign based on an ethical principle — that dumping industrial waste at sea was unacceptable — it had difficulties in the UK shaking off the accusation that its tactics were too emotive with marginalising the scientific aspects of the issue. While the Brent Spar case helped in focus attention on the campaign, it did give opposing forces the opportunity to criticise Greenpeace's stance as being unscientific. As a result, the focus shifted to the environmental implications of disposing of Brent Spar in the sea or by some other method, rather than addressing the broader issue of the dumping of industrial waste. This shift of agenda was probably the key development in the campaign. However, the organisation did not believe it affected the overall impact of its campaign because, even though the tone of the message was occasionally perceived as 'shrill', the public appeared to understand the central issue and were prepared to support Greenpeace on that basis.

The end of the campaign
One of the final acts in the campaign had been for Greenpeace to measure the amount of toxic waste on the platform. This measurement was found to be different to Shell's and Greenpeace accused the company of lying to the public. It was subsequently discovered that Greenpeace's measurement was wrong, which the

quickly admitted when it realised the mistake. Nonetheless, the error generated a concerted attack on Greenpeace from both the government and Shell and received wide coverage in the media.

The question of amounts of toxic waste, was not considered by Greenpeace to be central to its campaign, but the organisation nevertheless apologised to Shell for its mistake. For Greenpeace, the principle of dumping was the central theme, and the actual level of waste on Brent Spar a side issue.

However, the amount of toxic waste on Brent Spar did become a central issue and the organisation's apology was interpreted by the government and the media as an admission that it had not 'won fairly'. This perception has continued to create problems for Greenpeace, despite the broadly successful outcome of the campaign. Greenpeace Campaigns Director, Doug Parr, noted that a key lesson was learnt:

> *Never play on the opposition's territory...Always stick to your own framing of the issue...stick to your agenda. It's not exactly a new lesson...but when journalists come at you with a particular point of view you can get involved in their way of thinking about it, when in reality you have to say 'no, we don't actually agree with that...and its not important to our argument'...but telling them to sod off is quite difficult sometimes!*

Greenpeace did seek media coverage for the campaign, although this was seen as a means to an end and not an end in itself. The organisation also began to find that other industries were starting to understand that the products and waste they generated might also attract negative coverage. As a result, Greenpeace has found it much easier to talk to the business sector which has come to see the organisation as a serious player. In addition, the fact remains that Greenpeace has for the time being succeeded in stopping oil companies from dumping at sea — none of them wants to be saddled with the 'next Brent Spar'.

However, the campaign has also had less favourable effects for Greenpeace. Partly as a result of the error over measurements, the organisation now finds itself under closer scrutiny than before and is challenged more frequently by the media. There is also a feeling among much of the media, particularly from the BBC, that in some way it was 'hoodwinked' by the organisation. As a result, journalists are now less willing to approach Greenpeace for information.

This residue of bad feeling relates, in part, to the use of dramatic video footage supplied directly by Greenpeace. This was used by the media and gave television-news producers instant footage to illustrate this very visual story. In hindsight, the media felt that it had placed too much emphasis on Greenpeace sacrificing its own objectivity and creating an impression that the media was following the Greenpeace agenda. While Greenpeace can hardly be held responsible for the conduct of the media, its very success in getting coverage has in some ways backfired on the organisation.

The organisation has since faced difficulties in getting its message into the mainstream media and the effects of this were seen in the poor coverage received by a subsequent campaign on North Sea fishing. The Brent Spar campaign could be considered to have been an expensive exercise for an organisation which is so focused on shaping public attitudes and galvanising social change.

Postscript
A recent report from the international business consultancy group Control Risks reported that British firms are becoming increasingly sensitive about the consequences of being targeted in high-profile campaigns on environmental and human rights issues. Environmental groups were seen as being particularly successful in altering company policies. One in three British companies altered investment decisions due to human rights issues and 57 per cent of development directors of large companies expected the risks posed by pressure groups to increase over the next five years. It is interesting to note that 90 per cent of the businesses surveyed thought that it would be possible to work with pressure groups on the environment. The survey covered 51 global companies with a turnover in excess of £1 billion *(The Times, 13 January 1997)*.

USE OF LANGUAGE AND IMAGERY

The claims made by a campaign and the style in which they are pursued should be appropriate to the gravity of the issue and accurately reflect the evidence the organisation has. Many organisations have suffered a loss of credibility because campaign positions have been extrapolated from a limited number of cases or weak evidence. This can lead to a weakening of the case overall and a subsequent loss of support for the campaign, if not for the organisation itself. However, it is legitimate to 'create' a campaign based around a survey of members or client group's views, for example; in order to heighten awareness of an issue.

The language and imagery employed by a campaign should be relevant and appropriate for the organisation. Clearly, terms that are offensive or make inappropriate connotations should be avoided. Furthermore, while different campaigns demand different approaches, most organisations will want to maintain consistency in the types of imagery and language they use overall.

To address these issues, many organisations have developed guidelines on the use of imagery and language. Organisations representing people with disabilities, for example, have drawn up guidelines to ensure that the content of their campaigns does not denigrate disabled people or portray them in a passive or dependant way. Some campaigners have developed internal guidelines to be used throughout their organisations, as well as by supporters and members, to ensure that the entire organisation produces images which are not at odds with the campaign message or ethos of the parent body.

Oxfam, for example, has developed guidelines that are issued to members who will be campaigning. *Oxfam and Images* is designed to ensure that there is consistency between the images used and the aims of the organisation (see Figure 10).

Figure 10: Oxfam's Guidelines on Using Imagery

Before you start, think about the images you'll be creating or using in words or pictures.

Ask yourself: What is your objective? What sort of image are you creating?

- Would the subjects of that image want it to be used?
- Are they named? Do you know anything about them?
- Can you use their words with the image?
- If men and women are involved, who is doing what? Do their roles reinforce gender stereotypes?
- What is the apparent relationship between black and white people?
- How are people with disabilities portrayed?

If you are using a photograph...be careful!

- Photographs where the photographer looks down on the subject can make them feel dependant or vulnerable.
- Does a raised head lend dignity?
- Don't use pictures that portray women as sexual objects.
- Cropping a photo can change its meaning or context.
- Visual puns can slip in, leaving subjects open to ridicule. Ask others to check your photo in case you have missed something.
- The words accompanying the photo can make all the difference.

If it seems impossible to find an appropriate image:

- Could you use more images for balance?
- Would a different caption change the impact?
- Is there a better format which might solve the problem?

(Source: *Oxfam and Images*)

Organisations need to think about a process for establishing a code that is relevant to their aims in consultation with those the organisation represents. This can be done by sharing the guidelines with trustees, involving groups of users or beneficiaries in the construction of the messages or asking them to comment on the images that are being used. There are some basic rules that can be followed: many of them are encompassed by the Oxfam guidelines.

Save the Children went through a similar process and produced guidelines that are comparable but more specific:

Figure 11: Save the Children's Guidelines on Using Imagery

- The dignity of the people with whom Save the Children works should be preserved. The people with whom Save the Children works may be perceived by some as helpless recipients of hand-outs. Poverty and dependence are not characteristics of communities.
- The images of, and text used, in all communications must be accurate and should avoid stereotypes and clichés. Text and images selected solely for shock value can trivialise, distort or misrepresent the work of Save the Children. To evoke concern and stimulate interest and action, present facts and photographs accurately.
- The people with whom Save the Children works are active partners in development and not just the recipients of aid. Clarity in portraying these factors strengthens rather than weakens text and pictures.
- Disability takes many forms. Disabled people are an integral part of the community and should be seen that way. A person in a wheelchair is an over-used symbol of disability which reinforces rather than broadens society's common view of disability. Avoid using that image unless it is particularly appropriate to the situation.
- Ethnic groups, women and disabled people should not be excluded from the text or photographs that involve them.
- Careful consideration should be given to the language used to describe the people with whom Save the Children works, not only in terms of factual accuracy but also tone. Patronising, mawkishly sentimental or demeaning words or phrases should be avoided.
- Attempts should be made where possible to identify and quote the people being photographed or interviewed. If they want to remain anonymous, their request should be honoured.
- Text should be matched accurately with photographs... Text and photographs that present conflicting messages...should not be used.
- Images must not be cropped or edited in a way that distorts the accurate situation. Pictures of weak, sick or dying victims of famine or other disasters must not be used out of context.

(Source: *Save the Children*)

There are some general rules common to both of these and other organisations' guidelines that could be applicable to most groups. Campaigners should:

- use language and images that respect the people they work with;
- not use stereotypes and clichés in language or images, either of the people they work with or of others;
- try to use the language and words of those they are representing and avoid speaking for them wherever possible;
- always gain permission to use the images and words that appear in publications; ensure that the text matches with the image and that both reflect the principles that the organisation is trying to promote.

The tone of the language and imagery within a campaign will make a significant difference to the way that campaign is received; different styles and tone are often needed for different audiences and different types of campaigns. The language used in fundraising and other campaigns needs to reflect the urgency of the issue. Often it is also an appeal to action, so the tone may be urgent and sometimes confrontational. It is important to remember, however, that communications should also establish a dialogue, not only with potential supporters but also, through them, with the target of the campaign. It is important that the communication stays within the limits of the issue and that it allows for future dialogue with those who the campaign is trying to influence. Good campaigning is always an attempt to persuade (rather than bludgeon) an audience into seeing the merits of a case.

It is sometimes possible to use images that appeal to a wide section of the public yet still make a strong statement.

However, it may be that for the intended audience, especially if the appeal is to a traditional donor base, campaigns may have to start with propositions and imagery that relate to the audience's own perceptions of the issue and then, through a dialogue with supporters, develop these perceptions over a period of time. This may require sustained effort over many years, as the charity Barnardo's discovered. Their own research showed that 95% of people questioned in a MORI poll still thought they ran orphanages, yet Barnardo's closed its last children's home in 1981. (Marketing Business, June 1997, p.12)

It is important to test what the public's attitude is to the campaign issue. A picture can be built up from previous work done in the area but, given the resources, it is useful for campaigners to have objective information, from market research if possible, on how organisations are perceived and what the public already think about the issue.

For instance, although an organisation will know the details of its own campaign inside out, it must take into account any associated concerns or interests of the target group. This feedback will help the planners position the campaign and ensure that erroneous assumptions about the views or understanding of the target audience are avoided. This is especially necessary for campaigns seeking to change attitudes.

WWF International is a valuable example. It faces the problem of trying to raise environmental issues across a diverse range of countries with different attitudes to the environment and separate local issues.

Case Study
VIII. WWF International

MORI were commissioned by WWF International to conduct a programme of research into the general public's attitudes towards the environment and perceptions of environmental organisations in 15 countries. The objective of the research was to track the relevance of the environment as an issue for the populations of the various countries that WWF International was active in, in order to help the organisation to position its campaigning.

Among all the countries surveyed, researchers identified a basis of environmental concern which provided a starting point for WWF International to communicate its messages to the public. The destruction of tropical rainforests was the most often-cited global concern, partly reflecting previous media activity around the issue. Concern for the rainforest was followed by concern about global warming and pollution. However; when questioned in more detail, it became apparent that the respondents' main concerns were for their immediate environment rather than global environmental issues. Health – particularly children's health emerged as an important issue. Many of the local issues cited related to the quality of life respondents wanted. In this context, they then cited air pollution and noise pollution as key concerns. WWF International also found that, as well as the general themes respondents came up with, there were distinct national problems: in New Zealand nuclear testing came to the Fore, while in the South Pacific it was urban planning and development.

The major implication was that WWF International could not have one overall position or message for the different countries but that campaign communications had to take into account the preoccupations of the national audiences in order to obtain good results in each country.

In countries which had only become industrialised relatively recently there was general support for industrialisation and the perceived benefits it brought. Coupled with this came a decreased likelihood of respondents having carried out certain environmentally friendly activities. These countries also had the fewest environmental activists.

This led WWF International to develop different strategies for communicating environmental messages to countries where the awareness of environmental issues was relatively low. Five animated television advertisements were developed using light-hearted messages to convey the importance of improving individual environmental behaviour. One of these concentrates on the issue of consumption and demonstrates how individual consumption patterns can be altered to the benefit of the environment by switching off lights, using less water, and so on.

In contrast, the campaign for countries where environmental awareness was well-developed and activism already established was much more strident. Here WWF International was able to produce dramatic and hard-hitting television advertisements which discussed the organisation's tropical rainforest work and the importance of stopping rainforest destruction. One depicted a rare-woods table being sold at auction: 'This table contributed to global warming...Surely this must be worth something? This is the last table to come out of the rainforest'. Another advertisement shows trees in the rainforest falling one by one as the result of timber trade activities. As each falls, an illness is called out: 'Aids', 'Cancer', 'Malaria' and then the voice-over cuts in: 'The rainforest may hold the key to all these diseases — if there is any rainforest left.'

The different styles of the campaigns were developed as a direct result of the research on the profile of the issue and the levels of awareness of the audience. Polling can, thus, be an extremely powerful tool in establishing how a campaign can target a message in the most appropriate way to achieve the maximum effect.

HITTING ON THE RIGHT TONE AND STYLE

Most organisations will benefit from close consideration of what processes should be set up for checking and agreeing the style of a campaign. The following list illustrates some of the issues that may need to be addressed:

- In what way is the issue sensitive for the client group or members?
- What overall tone is wanted for the campaign. For example, should it be angry and challenging? Should it be humorous? Or should it appeal to people's softer sentiments?
- Does the organisation have any existing internal guidelines? Would it be appropriate to draw up guidelines in consultation with users and stakeholders?
- Can the organisation guarantee that publications and public statements will follow the tone set for the campaign and that the style will not conflict with

the message? Also, can it ensure that the campaign messages will not make claims that cannot be backed up by evidence?

- Can the organisation establish what the public perception of the issue is and how best can this be related to its communications?
- Are similar issues already the subject of public attention or debate; will a new campaign really break new ground?
- How controversial is the issue and how can the campaign take advantage of this controversiality without losing control of its message?
- If the organisation is a charity, do the tone and style of the campaign accord with the guidelines of the Charity Commission? (see Part 4).

THE LANGUAGE OF RIGHTS: BEWARE!

The language of rights has become the language of the voluntary sector. Much lip service is paid to the rights of those on whose behalf campaigns are launched. In recent years this has been extended to cover animals as well as people.

The language of rights has a powerful resonance in public debate but its use does need to be clarified. The continued use of the language of rights is in danger of devaluing the political currency of debate by trying to define everything within its orbit. The claim to rights becomes no more than a rhetorical device for trying to establish a claim to resources. However, the leverage rights language may have on the political debate becomes diluted when the public is bombarded with the next set of rights claims from yet another pressure group. The claims become devalued, and everyone becomes more cynical, including those whose rights are being advocated.

ADJUSTING PUBLIC POSITION

Public positioning determines the way an organisation relates to government, to those it might be seeking to influence, and to the organisation's own members. The Ramblers' Association made a deliberate attempt, during the course of a campaign to promote rights of access to the countryside, to modify its perceived image of being dominated by radical activists. The Association wanted a more responsible image in the eyes of government, with whom it was promoting its bill, and the Country Landowners Association, whose members felt threatened by the Association's stance. There was also evidence that some of the Association's members were being put off by the perceived militancy of the organisation (*Independent*, 11 February 1996).

The Association addressed a complex situation and deliberately changed its public positioning in order to increase credibility with government while reassuring the core of its members that the organisation was still worth supporting. While doing so, it also neutralised the negative influence of a potential opponent.

COMMUNICATING WITH THOSE YOU SERVE

The style of campaigning becomes especially important for organisations that provide services to those on whose behalf they are campaigning. Campaign images should portray members in a way which reflects their status as active participants. One of the best ways of ensuring that the messages and images used in a campaign are appropriate is holding regular consultations with the people an organisation represents in order to assess their views on the materials being used or developed.

This process can become complex in practice because of the different ways in which images and campaign themes can affect the public and users. A campaign run in the national press by a leading child-care organisation highlighting the problem of child abuse led the users of another service provided by the same agency to avoid a local centre for fear of being stigmatised as abusers! Organisations need to ensure that they have mechanisms in place to consult with service users about the images used to portray them. This can be done by monitoring feedback from users and the public, although this can be costly. This can also be done on a smaller scale, using, for example, focus groups of service users.

PUBLICATIONS

Publications of differing types can be the most visible form of a campaign. Careful thought needs to be given to the type of publication necessary to promote the campaign and particular consideration should be given to who the intended audience is. For some campaigns, magazines and newsletters are excellent means of building support, while, for others, leaflets and brochures or posters may be more suitable. Often, for some members of the public, the first contact they may have with a cause is through a leaflet summarising the aims of the campaign or inviting their participation.

Many of the larger voluntary sector organisations produce printed materials. The costs of such publications are, of course, prohibitive for small organisations for those who can afford them but there are considerable benefits:

- they are a simple and effective way of communicating with members and campaign supporters;
- they mobilise and inform supporters more effectively than other forms of communication;
- they attract new supporters and members;
- they are the most effective way of communicating new information about campaigns to members and supporters;
- they help to establish an organisation's credibility and profile.

The production of publications can also offer campaigners an opportunity to involve members and supporters by using them as a source for news stories, articles and photographs.

Organisations need to consider carefully their reasons for producing publications and the extent to which those materials are appropriate for the target groups. There are also some key questions to be addressed about the way the publications are going to be produced and funded.

The publication, *A Good Cause to Publish?*, issued by the Royal Mail (Cobb, 1996), identifies the main elements in the production of a publication:

WRITING, EDITING AND DESIGNING
While these can now be done on computer and sent direct to a reproduction house, there is still a high level of staff time and energy involved. Editing documents and copy can take time and is a considerable skill. The more copy that is written in-house, the more time it takes.

ILLUSTRATIONS
Photography agencies can provide you with pictures — at a price. Staff, members and other supporters may be able to take and use their own. There are also many freelance photographers, cartoonists and illustrators that can be commissioned for a reasonable fee.

PRINTING
Printing costs will vary with the technology used, quality and thickness of paper, and the supplier. The content of the publication also affects its cost, with the reproduction of photographs and any use of colour pushing costs up considerably. However, building up a relationship with two or three printers and asking for competitive quotes will help to limit expenses.

DISTRIBUTION
This adds considerably to costs. It is not just the cost of mailing that must be considered but also establishing and maintaining the circulation lists, although some organisations will be able to base these on donor or membership lists.

PROMOTION AND ADVERTISING
While organisations can use their publications to attract external advertising, they must also pay to advertise and promote the publications themselves . Even attracting advertising will require investment in sales staff or existing staff time. Advertising agencies can be used but will want commission at a standard rate of between 20-30 per cent. Subscription also involves the costs of renewals and maintaining the database.

Cost is an obvious consideration and campaign groups will need to assess the benefits of a publication versus other activity. However, given the visibility that publications can bring, they can often be useful vehicles for seeking sponsorship or for straight forward fundraising efforts. At a local level, local authorities or local businesses will sometimes consider supporting voluntary sector publishing initiatives. At a national level, provided there is no conflict of message, publications can be highly attractive to potential sponsors. Indeed, securing sponsorship can sometimes add to the credibility of the message through the association with a known and respected organisation. For organisations whose strategy would preclude association with certain groups of sponsors, publishing support can sometimes be secured from trusts and foundations with an interest in the topic.

PUBLICITY AND LOCAL CAMPAIGNING

Local campaigns employ a number of effective publicity tools. In determining the public profile of a campaign, the same general principles apply to local projects as to others.

One of the major tasks of local publicity is to promote the issues in a way that gives them immediacy for the community and encourages people to support – and involve themselves in – the campaign. Below are a number of common ways in which local issues are pursued.

LOCAL PRESS

The press need to be engaged by the use of relevant and interesting stories that will relate to local concerns. Many organisations use local celebrities, MPs or dignitaries to endorse their cause and get more publicity, although this can lead to conflict: when a community group used the fact that the local MP was also the Secretary of State for a major government department to get coverage in the four local papers some supporters thought that the campaign was compromised by having it associated with a government minister.

Campaigners need to assess how a high-profile figurehead may be perceived by a local audience: will personality involved detract from or enhance the message? A prominent comedian, for example, may not have the right profile for an issue needing a sensitive approach but may be the perfect choice for a publicity stunt.

Many national organisations provide specific guidance on the production of local media campaigns.

PETITIONS

Petitions are extensively used by local campaign groups to show the strength of feeling over a particular issue. These are a useful tool because the process of collecting signatures allows campaigners to talk to local people about the issue. Yet though petitions are a useful adjunct to the campaign they will not make up for a weak case. They should have clearly identified target recipients and should be timed to coincide with the relevant decision-making process. Local groups should also consider whether establishing the level of public concern will really help to achieve a favourable decision.

EVENTS
Events provide a local focus for organisations work and increase their profile. Campaigners should be clear about what they aim to achieve by staging events.

ELECTIONS
Local elections provide significant opportunities for groups to raise campaign issues and put pressure on elected representatives. Whether the group is a charity or not they must be careful not to contravene election law — see Part 4.

LETTER WRITING
Letter-writing campaigns are particularly effective and can mobilise group members. Many organisations have used postcards or other devices carrying specific messages as a simple way of raising issues with a large number of people. Organisations that are charities need be aware of the Charity Commission's guidelines in this area — see Part 4, Keep it Legal!.

CAMPAIGNING ON THE INTERNET
The 1996 party political conferences could be visited from anywhere in the world. All that was needed was a computer and a modem to enter the Virtual Party Conference exhibition. Visitors could tap into electronic versions of many of the exhibits, watch the conference proceedings via the television link, join in discussions via the conference bulletin board, order materials or send a fax complaining to the French Government about the destruction of the Muroroa atoll by atomic testing. The exhibition was a foretaste of the potential power of electronic communications for campaigners.

Looking towards the future, the winner of a recent Royal Institute of British Architects competition to design an extension to the Houses of Parliament was a design that proposed a virtual Parliament where constituents could visit their MPs without having to leave their living room, and MPs could conduct business without leaving their offices.

Reality is already catching up with this vision as many MPs can now be contacted via the World Wide Web and the electorate can enter into dialogue with them in a way that would not otherwise be possible. Party leaders have also taken part in open question-and-answer sessions on the Internet. Whether MPs can to continue to cope with the extra demands of being accessible via the Internet is another question.

The Internet has the potential to open new channels of communication for campaigners. Some of the main benefits for campaigners could include:

- involvement of people who find it difficult to attend meetings, such as people with disabilities and those living in rural areas;

- flexible format that can be altered quickly as events change, facilitating instant communication with other offices or members;
- the extension of communication to people from all over the world, especially relevant for an organisation like Amnesty International which conducts international letter-writing campaigns via a worldwide membership;
- the development of different forums of communication, especially at the level of community groups;
- access to House of Commons information on the progress of bills, parliamentary business and select committees;
- electronic publishing of reports and campaign information;
- easier access to decision makers;
- an improvement in the development of local activists who can be linked together and instantly updated on campaigns.

The Internet can be a great leveller. A small community group can have the same size home page as the largest multi-national. The Internet has been used effectively in such campaigns as that launched by Greenpeace on the Brent Spar through to the McLibel campaign in which two individuals were sued by McDonalds for allegations they made about the environmental impact of the company's trading practices. Much of that campaign's impact came from the way the defendants were able to mobilise support and activity around the world targeted at a major international company from their own web page. However these advantages are offset by the fact that many people have no access to the Internet or computers. This may be the new face of democracy - but it's only for those who can afford the technology.

All of these uses are being tested by campaigning organisations. However there is danger in exaggerating the impact of new technologies. The development of cheap personal computing allowed many national and community groups to take advantage of powerful database and word-processing programmes to target MPs and business with letter-writing campaigns. It did not take long for this tactic to be discredited as anything but a very rough or even false guide to public opinion as the targets saw through the mass-produced nature of the communication.

A similar risk of information overload exists in the development of the Internet as a campaigning tool. Furthermore, there is a danger that the increased access to decision makers offered to those organisations able to afford the new communication technologies will widen the gap between those with the resources to access to the new technology and those who do not.

7.

Effective Fundraising through Campaigns

JOINT CAMPAIGNS

The relationship between fundraising and campaigning often follows one of two patterns: Firstly, some campaigns integrate core fundraising objectives with policy or issue campaigning objectives. Such integrated campaigns aimed at different audiences will require separate success criteria. Secondly, some campaigning initiatives, particularly those undertaken by small organisations, require an element of fundraising at an early stage simply to enable the main thrust of the campaign to take place. The history of voluntary sector campaigning is littered with examples of projects that have never left the drawing board due to lack of funds. Campaigns are also at risk of failure when they are designed around predetermined notions of style rather than based on a realistic assessment of resources and a careful consideration of the strategies most likely to achieve the desired objectives.

Large budgets are not required for successful campaigning. Some of the voluntary sector's most successful campaigns have been run on shoestring budgets and many commercial public relations and lobbying agencies have voiced amazement at the success of campaigns managed on resources a tenth of those they would conventionally deploy.

CAMPAIGN FUNDING

The issue of how to raise funds for campaigns is beyond the scope of this book. There are many sources of information on the subject as well as professional fundraisers who can be consulted for advice, through the Institute of Charity Fundraising Managers, for example. Nevertheless, the availability of funds and other resources is fundamental to most campaigns and there are a number of factors to consider:

- Does your organisation wish to base its campaign on available funds, or to set the campaign objectives first and then seek appropriate funding?
- Is there sufficient funding available before the launch of the campaign to avoid the risk of a funding crisis mid-campaign?
- Are all those involved in fundraising aware of legal restrictions such as the 1992 Charities Act, regulations governing street collections and raffles and the like?
- Have you prepared a proper assessment of fundraising potential to ensure that your expectations are realistic?
- Have you briefed and prepared campaign supporters who can often be a good starting point for helping to raise funds or making personal donations?
- Have you sought non-monetary support, such as free advertising space or printing, or the use of facilities such as a photocopier or office?
- Have you approached advertising, PR or public affairs agencies to provide free advice or services?
- Have you effectively used fundraising activities to motivate and involve supporters in the campaign?

CAMPAIGN RESOURCES

Critical to many campaigns is the availability of resources. The history of voluntary sector campaigning is littered with examples of projects that have never left the drawing board due to lack of funds. Campaigns are also at risk of failure if they are designed around predetermined notions of the style rather than based on a realistic assessment of resources and a careful consideration of the strategies most likely to achieve the desired objectives.

Some of the voluntary sector's most successful campaigns have been achieved on shoestring budgets and many commercial public-relations and lobbying agencies have voiced amazement at the success of campaigns achieved on resources a tenth of those they would conventionally deploy.

In raising funds for campaigns there are a number of potential sources to be considered:

- Campaign supporters are always the first port of call for any campaign funding — while the campaign itself may be about an absence of funding for a service, there are often other people supporters can approach.
- Other voluntary organisations, or potential alliance partners.
- Running events, either small-scale ones like flag days, jumble sales, sponsored walks, etc., or more ambitious projects such as galas, balls and supported premieres.
- Trusts and foundations with an interest in the area.
- Commercial companies — many local and national companies will consider supporting campaigns where there is a relevant link.

- Local authorities.
- Central government grant schemes — a number of departments have grant programmes for voluntary organisations and some consider support for campaigns to raise public awareness.
- The National Lottery — the lottery distribution boards, especially the National Lottery Charities Board, can, depending on their programmes, provide funding for particular campaigns.

In addition to seeking funds, campaigning organisations should also consider appealing for forms of non-monetary support, which can be equally as helpful. Sometimes, rather than asking for money, making an approach for advice or free advertising space can be successful. For example, during a campaign run by a well-known charity to change government policy, the charity benefited from £25,000 free national advertising space in a deal negotiated by a friendly advertising agency.

In addition, advertising, PR or public-affairs agencies are sometimes willing to provide free advice or consultancy, or indeed to seek free support from their own contacts. One or two hours free consultation with an 'expert' in the field can save an organisation many days of work.

Such free gifts in time or in kind are not limited to national organisations. Many local campaigns have benefited from local businesses giving access to free photocopying and printing, and often local newspapers as well as being helpful advocates can provide discounted or free advertising space, sometimes even 'adopting' a campaign.

The key to all fundraising for campaigns is 'if you don't ask, you don't get'. Critical to campaign fundraising is the drawing up of the campaign plan; what resources are required, are they easily obtainable, and who has the contacts to reach them?

Campaigners need to draw up a list of potential sources and note the strengths and weaknesses of each. For example, in the case of commercial sponsorship, while the potential for acquiring considerable funds may appear attractive, it may be too time consuming to realise and there may be a risk that a sponsor will seek to place conditions on a campaign. In the case of fundraising from central or local government, questions to be considered include the appropriateness of the source and the timescale for decisions.

Once such a listing has been undertaken and appropriate sources decided upon, as with any fundraising exercise an action plan needs to be developed. Of prime importance will be the form of approach to be made — will it be by letter, will it require the setting up of a campaign fundraising sub-committee; and who will make the approach?

While fundraising is often subject to intuition as well as judgement, there are a number of issues about fundraising for campaigns that require consideration. Campaigners need to ask themselves:

- Is a successful fundraising exercise critical to the conduct of the campaign?
- Does the launch of the campaign need postponing until the necessary funds are acquired?
- Is it better to delay fundraising until tangible success in the campaign is achieved in order to demonstrate to potential funders the role of the campaign?

Is fundraising a good way to get people involved in the campaign?

Campaigners also need to ensure that fundraising requirements are considered early enough in a campaign plan; diverting campaigns in midstream to fundraising activities can have an adverse impact on progress and can cause a campaign to run out of steam.

Funders are not simply passive objects. Keeping them informed of progress can make them more amenable to future requests and builds on their loyalty. Furthermore, while most people like to be associated with success, not every campaign succeeds, and funders are more likely to feel well disposed towards a failed campaign if they know the reasons for its failure.

Fundraising for charities is subject to certain legal restrictions arising out of the 1992 Charities Act. It is important that the relevant requirements of the Act and the recommendations on good practice from the Institute of Charity Fundraising Managers are observed. It can be very damaging for an organisation if a campaign attracts bad publicity, and scores an own goal, because of a failure to observe such regulations.

While campaigning often relies on fundraising, the relationship between the two functions within organisations is one that can produce tension and lead to a sense of lost opportunity. There is considerable debate about how well campaigning and fundraising messages can be integrated and much depends on how an organisation is positioned, who its donors are and the relationship it has with them.

While it is clear that all organisations appealing for funds will do their best to state a strong case for their needs, there are often significant differences in the way fundraisers and campaigners approach the communication of a message. Related to this, the supporters that contribute to fundraising appeals are often not motivated by the same issues and approaches that appeal to staff campaigners. However, the extent of these divisions will vary enormously from organisation to organisation and from issue to issue.

Clearly, while some organisations will have dedicated fundraising and campaigning teams, the same will not necessarily apply in small or local organisations. Local campaigns frequently spring from a need to raise funds for specific projects and fundraising is often the public's first point of contact with a voluntary organisation.

While it will not always be appropriate or possible to run joint projects, it clearly makes sense to ensure that campaigning and fundraising activities do not promote widely divergent images of an organisation and contain different or contradictory messages.

The housing charity Shelter has developed a checklist of actions to promote closer co-operation between fundraisers and campaigners. This grew out of campaign activity which successfully attempted to combine fundraising and campaigning approaches.

Figure 12: Checklist for fundraisers and campaigners

The following questions are designed to help organisations evaluate how effective the partnership is between their fundraising and campaigning teams:

Internal
- Do the teams meet regularly (informally and formally)?
- Do the heads of the fundraising and campaigns teams meet regularly, discuss issues of common interest and explore opportunities for partnership?
- Does the Chief Executive support closer working relationships between campaigning and fundraising?
- What system is there for checking that service users or others the organisation represents are comfortable with the imagery and materials being used?

Looking at supporters
- Does the organisation's database contain donors or supporters (see below)?
- Does the organisation's campaign team have its own database of campaigners? (This may be a barrier to an integrated approach.)
- Does the organisation use supporters who give money as a campaigning resource?

Effective Use of Direct Marketing
- Does the organisation use direct marketing techniques in campaigning and are the skills and facilities used by the fundraising team also used by the campaign team?
- Does the organisation ask supporters to do more than give money and buy merchandise?
- Is it possible to identify supporter records to show an interest in campaigning, any actions they may have taken or interests they may have?
- Does the organisation use a direct-marketing agency? How would it respond to requests to present ideas on ways of adopting campaigning as part of an integrated campaign and fundraising strategy?

Regulatory Environment
- Does the organisation fully understand the limits set on campaigning and fundraising by the Charity Commission guidelines and other recommendations? (see Part 4)
- Does the organisation have a formal system of checking that the materials used will meet the guidelines, and is this applied to all communications?

The principal elements of this checklist were developed as part of an ongoing attempt by Shelter to combine fundraising with the recruitment of campaign supporters. While specific to the circumstances faced by Shelter, that organisation's experience provides an interesting case study of the way in which the approaches of direct marketing and the issues of campaigning can be brought together.

Case Study
VIII. The Doomsday Campaign

In February 1994, the government launched its Housing Green Paper. It was argued that the proposals it contained would drastically reduce the rights of homeless people. In support of a wider campaign undertaken by more than 80 organisations, Shelter produced The Doomsday Campaign. The campaign consisted of press advertisements, action packs to mailout, an emergency direct mail shot calling for funds and a telemarketing drive to key segments of the donor database who were approached with a specific request to contact the Housing Minister. The aim of this activity was to produce enough public pressure on the government to get the proposals shelved while using the opportunity to extend the recruitment of donors who could also take campaign action.

To a significant extent, the success of the strategy depended on how many of those contacted were prepared to take some kind of action. Shelter selected those who had responded positively to a previous mailing which had featured parliamentary work and those who had been recruited via projects with a campaigning bias such as the New Internationalist. New fields were then set up on Shelter's database to record commitments made and any actions taken, such as writing to the Department of the Environment.

The results exceeded the campaigners' expectations. The principal achievements were:

- the largest response to a Green Paper Shelter had ever achieved, with over 10,000 letters to the Minister, 3,000 of these from donors and advertisement respondents;
- the donor appeal was the most successful ever in financial terms and telemarketing sheets showed that donors had been happy to be asked to do more than just give money;
- the proposals in the Green Paper were shelved for 12 months.

The main lessons learned from the first part of the campaign were that:

- it was important to tailor the database to capture the name of donors who had expressed an interest in campaigning;
- campaigning involvement can bring donors closer to the organisation - and boost the lifetime value of donations;
- campaign supporters are motivated differently from fundraising respondents, but not that differently. Appropriate targeting of campaign messages, together with segmentation of the database, did work.

The following year the government returned to its agenda and the proposals re-emerged in the 1995 White Paper and then the Queen's Speech. The focus of the campaign then shifted to parliamentary lobbying. The main strategy was to recruit supporters to put pressure on the government during the campaign by writing letters and taking part in the parliamentary lobbying. An attempt was made to use the supporter base at key moments during the parliamentary campaign. Press advertising and an attitude survey recruited people who were prepared to take action as well as give money. A donor appeal and telemarketing was also used to raise funds for the parliamentary lobbying.

The result was that:

- 1,000 supporters came to a lobby;
- 4,000 letters were written to MPs who raised the issue with the Minister;
- an appeal was circulated to all donors — the first in many years — with the proposition that Shelter had to build up its campaigning funds to protect the funding of services for homeless people. The appeal exceeded its target by 40%.

During the passage of the bill, Shelter needed to produce pressure at a crucial moment to force an amendment. The aim of the campaign was to get 30-40 letters to each MP in an attempt to influence his or her vote. Telemarketing was chosen as the route to achieve this and Shelter contacted donors on a constituency basis. More than 70% agreed to help while only 1% objected to the action. Most importantly, half the campaign was handled by in-house workers including service-delivery staff, campaigners and fundraisers. This helped to cement the co-operation between different parts of the organisation.

(Source: based on material sent by Shelter prepared for an ICFM conference presentation, 1996, by John Trampleasure, Director of Marketing and Tim Hunter, Head of Marketing and Acting Head of Campaigns.)

IN CONCLUSION

Some key points emerge from this discussion:

- combining fundraising and campaigning messages successfully, requires the campaign to be based on an issue that has the capacity to engage supporters;
- funding for the campaign needs to be considered as an important part of the campaign strategy;
- clear actions which are simple, achievable and measurable must be identified;
- systems need to be in place to deal with the enquiries and complaints that such an approach might generate;
- involvement needs to be built over time around a clear proposition;
- clear systems for checking materials and involving trustees need to be present to ensure an appropriate style is maintained and that the campaign conforms with the Charity Commission's guidelines;
- the style and tone of the subject matter need to be appropriate to the issue and show respect to those concerned;
- campaigns and fundraising benefit by examining ways in which supporters can be involved in campaign issues.

The way an organisation positions itself will have a significant effect on the prospects of achieving a successful end to a campaign, retaining and increasing an organisation's support and influencing the perception its own members and stakeholders have of the organisation. Campaigners cannot afford to ignore these issues.

Part 3.
Evaluating Campaign Effectiveness

8.

Why Evaluate?

'I am told we won the campaign. Next time I would like to win the election.'
(John Prescott, following Labour's defeat in the 1992 General Election.)

'The only point of any campaign is to win the election.'
(Brendan Bruce responding to Peter Mandelson's claim that the Labour Party won the 1992 Election campaign).

Few situations are as clear cut as a general election. As John Prescott's assessment of the 1992 election shows, it is no use claiming that the campaign was won if the objective was not achieved. Campaigns however are rarely clear cut successes or failures. Much depends on the point at which the achievements are measured against the objectives of a campaign. While formal evaluation of charitable activity in general has been on the increase, less attention has been given to evaluating the impact of campaigning activities.

As Lord Nathan noted in his report 1990 on voluntary sector effectiveness, voluntary organisations have been slow to adopt the standard tools of management, which are used widely in the commercial and increasingly in the public sector.

Furthermore, as the report also notes, evaluation is crucial to accountability:

> *In no area of voluntary action, Lord Nathan writes, is open accountability more important than in campaigning...Moreover, an honest explanation of how money has been used to pursue campaigning goals, and to what effect, is a prerequisite for the good reputation of the voluntary organisations. It is also the best defence against misrepresentation by the political and vested interests which they are sometimes bound to upset.*

Good evaluation is vital for teams and organisations that want to improve performance. It helps focus the aims of the organisation's activities and keeps a clear sense of the ends and values they are trying to achieve. Evaluation is also a method of monitoring the way campaign activities measure up against an organisation's core values. In this way, evaluation may challenge the current resource allocation within an organisation in favour of campaigning as a better way of achieving those objects.

THE SPECIAL EVALUATION NEEDS OF VOLUNTARY ORGANISATIONS

The process of evaluation is very simple:

- select evaluation methods
- agree criteria for evaluation
- collect the evidence
- review against the agreed criteria
- write report
- share lessons with relevant audiences
- implement recommendations

Nevertheless, it is important to recognise some of the particular difficulties in evaluating campaigning:

- campaigns rarely start with a blank sheet which is to say that most issues have a history which effects the campaign outcome;
- when working in alliances it is often impossible to pinpoint who was responsible for a particular change;
- most campaigning takes place in a complex government and public-policy environment where it is difficult to disentangle the effects of any particular activity from the other influences upon decision makers;
- government and other agencies are not always open about the reasons for changes in policy or legislation and may in fact wish to hide the real reasons for changing their position;
- evaluation is never neutral within an organisation but part of a process of allocation or justification of resources;
- there are often concerns about the cost of evaluation when organisational resources are already likely to be stretched.

Many of the organisations interviewed for *The Good Campaigns Guide* survey monitored the political environment in which they were operating very closely and were aware of the effects of their campaigning on that level. However, there was uncertainty about the ways in which evaluation of campaign *activity* could best be carried out. Some organisations have developed evaluation frameworks with some success while others have appointed staff trained in evaluation techniques. While most of the respondents to the survey recognised the value of evaluation, some were less sure about how some of the traditional evaluation techniques could be applied where there was a high degree of uncertainty about the consequences of campaign activity in a complex political environment. All of the organisations interviewed recognised the importance of evaluating the work they did and a number of them indicated that, as a result of recent campaigning, they were intending to implement more formal procedures.

The RSPCA (see case study I) continued to monitor media and parliamentary support following its campaign for the Wild Mammals Protection bill (see Chapter 1) but no formal evaluation was undertaken. However, according to the organisation does have plans to introduce a formal evaluation process for future campaigns. The RSPCA acknowledged that the campaign had been well planned and executed and some valuable lessons had been learned which should be recorded and used for the development of future campaigns.

Transport 2000 put a strong emphasis on evaluation. The Director, Stephen Joseph, commented that 'Evaluation via the staff strategy meetings is critical from Transport 2000's point of view for working out what the priorities are for future campaigns'.

Amnesty International also put great stress on the value of evaluation. Looking at the Ken Saro Wiwa action, Rob Beasley, Campaigns Co-ordinator noted:

> For us, it's about breaking the campaign down, looking at the objectives and seeing what you have achieved. For the Ken Saro Wiwa campaign the objectives were quite straightforward, for others they are more complex. You know sometimes that you are building towards long-term objectives which you may not necessarily achieve, but on the way you have short- to medium-term ones. You do your evaluation by measuring how far you have got towards each of these.

The different approaches organisations took to evaluation were determined by their size. Small organisations relied upon the assessment of the campaign staff directly involved and in some cases the trustees who were actively engaged in a campaign. For example, Families Need Fathers did not conduct a formal evaluation of its campaign to change the rules around the Child Support Agency's operations, although its members had a clear idea of the achievements of the campaign. As the board are heavily involved in operational as well as strategic matters within this organisation (because it has only one staff member) it was felt that information on changes to strategy and tactics were readily available.

Different evaluation strategies will be appropriate to different sizes of organisation and different types of campaign but all organisations need to have in place at least a basic evaluation system. As Lord Nathan put it:

> We believe that the trustees of each voluntary organisation...have a responsibility, within the context of their objectives and powers, to review regularly whether the proportion of effort and resources

Figure 13: Process evaluation

Issue	Relevant questions	Measured by
Internal organisation	Were the campaign teams clear about the objectives of the campaign, were appropriate support structures in place — meetings, communication systems with other departments to ensure that staff could work effectively, etc.?	• Were priorities and actions for campaign clear and agreed? • Were these then stuck to? If not was this a valid choice? • Did staff have clear lines of communication to other parts of the organisation?
Conduct of the research	Was it done to time and did it produce evidence that was relevant to the campaign? Did it change the nature of the campaign?	• Research on time, level of usage by targeted audience; • Relevance to campaign materials being produced judged by staff evaluation or recipients; • Ability to generate a campaign from the evidence as assessed by campaign staff.
Briefing papers	Were these to time and relevant for the campaign? Did the recipients of the briefings receive them in time and were they used by them?	• MPs or other targets get briefings in time to be used, briefings used in a timely and appropriate way that is relevant to the campaign; • For example, MPs quote or demonstrably use the briefing in a debate or the press release is used to generate a story; • Surveys of MPs opinions on the issue (see section on Opinion Polls).
Materials	Were the materials adequate for pursuing the campaign?	• Number and quality of the materials produced; were they to time, were there enough for the members, level of demand?

Figure 13: continued

Issue	Relevant questions	Measured by
Responses to government	How long did it take to respond to requests for information? What was the quality of the information?	• That responses were delivered to deadlines. • Civil servants give positive feedback of the appropriateness of the information.
Responses to members	How long did it take to respond to requests for information? What was the quality of the information?	• Establish and measure a relevant timescale for responses; • Survey membership to establish if information was timely and useful; • Was it used by the members to communicate with the targets of the campaign.
Activity generated	Who took campaign actions and when?	• Numbers of members responding to campaigning requests; • Use of materials, number of campaign events delivered; • Number of signatures on petitions, level of involvement in other campaign; activities such as attendance at national or regional campaign events or conferences.
Media	What attempts were made to communicate with the media and were these timely?	• Number of press releases, level of contact with the media, number of mentions in the press, positioning of those mentions, e.g. front page; • Number of column inches and content of story; • Extent to which the media followed campaign agenda or vice versa; • Level of negative coverage or opposition engendered, spread of stories between national and local media. Did identified targets take the story?

directed to campaigning, as opposed to services or other tasks,
represents the most efficient mix of resources.

Evaluation is difficult unless the campaign had some clearly stated objectives and specified actions to achieve those objectives. Evaluations will also vary depending on *what* is being measured and the context of the evaluation. Distinctions often need to be made between long- and short-term objectives. Many organisations will have long-term objectives in relation to a campaign issue that will not be achievable within the term of a single project. It is important in evaluation and campaign planning to separate out different levels of objectives and assess how achievable the different targets of a campaign are. This will allow a realistic assessment of campaign priorities and the actions necessary to achieve them.

APPROACHES TO EVALUATION

Any system of monitoring or evaluation will require careful adaptation to the circumstances of an organisation and a campaign and there are many models of evaluation that could be followed. Four related approaches are outlined below: process evaluation, impact evaluation, gap analysis and comparative evaluation.

PROCESS EVALUATION

Process evaluation attempts to measure the activities undertaken during the course of a campaign to ensure that they have been implemented in the appropriate way and have obtained the desired effect. It assumes that the actions or methods used were the right ones and simply attempts to measure how far they have been carried out. It creates a baseline against which to judge the efficiency and timeliness with which an agreed set of actions were implemented. It does not attempt to measure whether the final aims of the campaign were achieved. It is important to pose the right questions regarding each activity or the wrong things may get measured. Figure 13 illustrates some typical types of activity that could be measured against a campaign plan.

Process evaluations can be especially useful where the outcome of a campaign is difficult to measure. By analysing the actions taken and the effect they have on the targets of the campaign, evaluations can be used where it is not possible to identify the specific actions that lead to a campaign success.

Even when a campaign has not achieved its aims, evaluation may often help explain why staff and supporters feel that the message has been put across well and the profile of the issue raised. This is one of the reasons why organisations need clear milestones within the planning of a campaign that can indicate whether objectives are being reached. These can include:

- public support for the issue increased by x per cent;

Figure 14: Impact evaluation

Type of change	Relevant questions	Measured by
Legislation	What changes have been made to legislation in line with the objectives in the campaign?	• Changes to the legislation, adoption of amendments, changes to regulations and guidance; • Statements from the Minister about future government intentions on the measure lobbied on.
Policy	What changes have been made to the policy and with what effect?	• Specific changes to policy reflected in government documents or pronouncements; • Funding for changes in line with these new commitments; • Promise to bring forward changes in legislation policy or practice; • Change in the terms of debate around the campaign issue measured by coverage in media, debates in Parliament or policy journals.
Practice	What evidence is there of changes to practice and how are these changes to take effect?	• Changes in the practice of agencies such as withdrawal of charges for a service, a change to assessment procedures, changes in the way the countryside is managed, etc.; • Changes in professional practice by agencies, such as the introduction of a new system of handling complaints.
Public attitude	What are the shifts in public perception of the campaign's target groups?	• Shifts in public perception of the issue measured against perceptions before the campaign started or against a control group not exposed to the campaign; • Number of people aware of the campaign message — focus groups can be used for an in-depth analysis of the impact of the campaign; • Change in behaviour from the target group following from the campaign.

- number of MPs supporting an Early Day Motion has reached x number;
- number and size of campaign meetings held;
- membership of organisation increased by x per cent;
- the amount of press coverage obtained;
- number of meetings with ministers and MPs held;
- use made of information by key public figures.

These are not a substitute for measuring the final outcome of a campaign but can help to evaluate how far a project is building pressure towards obtaining the desired outcome. The danger with process evaluation, if there is one, is that campaign activity may be confused with campaign goals. In this case an organisation could end up winning the campaign but losing the election!

IMPACT EVALUATION

There are a number of different elements to assessing the impact of a particular campaign. It is crucial to compare the effect of the actions taken with the stated aims and objectives of the campaign (see Chapter 1 on planning a campaign). A campaign may have unintended consequences that prove to be beneficial but it is important to establish yardsticks against which to measure the effect of campaign activities. The aim of impact evaluation is to asses the effect that campaign activity has in achieving campaign aims. Figure 14 below explores the process of impact evaluation.

An impact evaluation analysis should be able to pinpoint the relationship between the actions undertaken and the impact of the campaign. This will always be difficult and contentious where campaigning is concerned. A number of influences may be at play in any situation and many 'historic victories' have been won with the tacit collusion of government ministers fighting their own battles with the Treasury and using the influence of the lobby to strengthen their own positions. Any experienced campaigner will have been faced with a number of similar circumstances. However, the advantages of process and impact evaluation are that they can at least illuminate a number of actions and effects, and assign causes to these, based on the evidence and a certain amount of judgement.

GAP ANALYSIS

Gap analysis attempts to measure the discrepancy between the stated aims of a campaign, the actions taken and the outcomes. Process and impact evaluation can gather the information needed to identify such gaps which can then be measured. Gap analysis can also be used for ongoing campaigns. For example, if an organisation has the aim of maintaining a high level of contact with

Ministers and MPs but, when it monitors the actual level of activity in relation to that aim, it finds out that contact is only made with these targets on a sporadic basis, then the difference between what is actually happening and the campaign aim is the gap that needs to be addressed. The same process can be applied to other areas of activity. If the aim of a campaign depends upon a large volume of public support but few actions have been undertaken to achieve this, then gap analysis can identify the discrepancy that needs addressing.

The Royal Society for the Protection of Birds (RSPB) has produced an evaluation framework that seeks to measure both process and outcomes. The outcomes checklist includes:

- policy changes
- policy audience actions
- public awareness of RSPB
- public awareness of campaigns
- income generation
- membership recruitment
- supporter development

The guidance notes make it clear that it is necessary to define the outcomes that should be achieved at the start of a campaign and encourage members to use those outcomes to clarify what these should be. These can then be split into primary objectives, such as the achievement of policy goals, and secondary objectives, such as an increase in supporters. Campaigners are then encouraged to set targets for each area of activity and relate these to what can realistically be achieved and measured.

Importantly, RSPB asks evaluators to describe the difference between the predicted outcomes of the campaign and the actual achievement (Gap Analysis). In addition, they are asked to name the factors that they think account for the differences, such as failures of communication, failure to undertake planned campaign actions, external influences such as timescale, political factors or other pressures. The guidelines also suggest that it might be helpful to track these factors and attempt, where possible, to anticipate them in campaign planning and assess their effect as part of the evaluation.

COMPARATIVE EVALUATION

Another useful yardstick for campaigning organisations can be what other bodies in the sector are doing or how they are performing. In the business sector this is known as bench-marking and is used to establish relevant standards by reference to a leading organisation in the sector. While success in campaigning may be more difficult to measure, the same principles apply.

Comparative evaluation can take three forms:

- A general strategic survey in which the campaigning position of an organisation is reviewed against the environment it operates in, the positioning of other campaigners in the sector and the possibility for further action. The aim is not to assess how well an organisation is doing something but whether it should be engaged in that activity in the first place. This is especially important when an organisation has limited resources and there are a number of other pressure groups campaigning on similar issues. The aim of comparative evaluation here would be to identify the unique contribution that the organisation could bring to a campaign or to identify what kind of alliances could be formed.
- Comparison against similar campaigning agencies to see what their procedures and practices are, what methods they use to motivate supporters, how they plan and implement campaigns and how they allocate resources among campaign priorities. The success of such an evaluation will normally depend upon campaigners having access to a friendly source within another relevant organisation. It might also take the form of a peer group review conducted by a campaigns manager from a different charity.
- Review of campaign methods used by a similar agency that specifically looks at campaign techniques and assesses how appropriate they are for the organisation. For example, a campaign group that has little experience of involving members in its campaign activities could study and use the experiences of a similar organisation with an active membership.

EVALUATING MEDIA COVERAGE

Evaluating media coverage can be an extremely difficult task for campaigners. While it is easy to count the occurrences of coverage and relate these to a particular activity — a press release, a stunt, the launch of a report — it is more difficult to evaluate the effect that coverage has on the audience. Press work can be measured by process criteria (how much coverage for what kind of effort) or by impact criteria (what kind of effect with what kind of outcome). This second area is inherently the most difficult because it will always depend to some extent on subjective judgements.

Campaigners can compare the content of a story and the way the media have positioned an issue with the original intentions of a campaign. For example, if the aims of a campaign were to get a particular message across, then the monitoring of media coverage should evaluate the way the message was treated and what response it generated. When making an evaluation it is important for campaigners to recognise that media messages are not heard in isolation and the opposition's message is likely to have had an equal airing. Thus, the campaign by Families Need Fathers against the establishment of the Child Support Agency was countered by the media presence of those who supported the CSA. Evaluation of media coverage, then, has less to do with how much coverage was gained than it does with the *balance* of that coverage and how the arguments for each side where treated.

Areas to evaluate:

- amount of coverage — number of mentions or use of material;
- medium of coverage — press, radio, television;
- positioning of story — front page or inside, on the specialist pages, general news, feature article or editorial; documentary or broadcast news; daytime magazine or primetime current affairs programme. How does this compare with the original intention? For example, if the aim was to position a story as a general news story but it is treated as a special interest story than this could be viewed as a partial failure to break out of a stereotyped or marginal positioning by the media;
- balance of coverage between national and local;
- size of audience and audience profile of the media outlet;
- balance of the coverage within a particular story and overall within the campaign;
- success of follow up contact with journalists to get their reaction to the story and how it was positioned.

Sometimes an organisation aims to influence the terms of debate without being associated with a specific view. In this case, campaign evaluation must measure any shift in opinion that has occurred without making reference to the organisation, for example, a positive leader article in the press supporting the campaign's viewpoint.

An analysis of media coverage clearly needs to be integrated into an assessment of the impact of a campaign as a whole as press work is rarely the end result of a campaign but merely a means to an end.

9.

WHEN - AND WHAT - TO EVALUATE

Choosing between campaigning priorities is always a difficult process. Evaluation can help to show where the strengths of a particular organisation lie and where its energies would best be spent. Evaluations need to cover all aspects of a campaign. If the evaluation focuses on just one element, the results will be misleading. Crucially, evaluation should relate to the original objectives of the campaign and be a tool for improving future work. As Doug Parr, Campaigns Director of Greenpeace explained, evaluation work is useful when it is both timely appropriate to the campaign:

> There was an international evaluation done [focusing on what had gone wrong at the end of the Brent Spar campaign] which I think everyone recognised afterwards was a pretty stupid thing to have done. If you really want to evaluate a campaign, you have to understand [the mistakes] in the context of everything else that was going on.

No further evaluation was attempted because,

> 'people move on and their memories fade, and anyway you can spend a lot of time evaluating and not get much out of it, although that's not to say that you shouldn't do it'

The timing and costs of evaluation are also likely to be issues. However, the context for evaluating all voluntary sector activity is changing and organisations need to understand what this means for their campaigning efforts. Much more interest is being shown in a 'total quality management approach' where targets are built into the work programme and performance is continually checked against them with the aim of achieving continued improvement. Such programmes have the advantage of keeping the control and responsibility with the staff that have to implement the changes.

Evaluation should be distinct from staff performance review. Given the complexity of the exercise it would be even more difficult to maintain objectivity and reassure workers if evaluation was directly linked to staff appraisal or performance-related pay. From an organisational perspective, the evaluation process is inherently political yet this does not mean that it cannot be done without a level of objectivity.

Volunteers and members of local groups can also be good sources of feedback when organisations are conducting campaign evaluations as they are frequently the people who put strategy into practice. It can also be possible to obtain valuable information on the effectiveness of campaign materials and tactics from campaign targets such as donors.

WHO SHOULD EVALUATE?

Organisations can use a number of different people or agencies to evaluate campaigns.

INTERNAL EVALUATORS

Staff teams can perform a self-evaluation against process and impact criteria. According to Doug Parr Greenpeace ensures that campaign teams do a self evaluation: 'Teams of six or seven people who work directly on each project sit around a table and think "how did it go?" in a facilitated discussion'. The results of this discussion are then written up and circulated to other stakeholders in the project such as staff or volunteers who have been involved at some stage, for their comments. Following this, a full report is submitted to the senior management team and the Director who will decide upon appropriate action as a result. For larger campaigns this is supplemented by interviews and a report written for the Director and the board. For international campaigns, evaluations are conducted internationally.

A number of organisations now employ quality assurance or audit staff who support the organisation in evaluating its activities. They carry out their evaluations inside the organisation and benefit from understanding organisational sensitivities though they maintain a level of detachment. The main focus of an internal audit staff will be to develop evaluation tools for campaigners and give them support in putting these into practice. Another option would be to employ a qualified consultant to set up such a system for internal staff to use.

EXTERNAL EVALUATORS

An external evaluator can be brought in to review a campaign against a number of criteria established by the organisation. Alternatively, a campaign manger from a different organisation can be asked to review a campaign and offer an analysis of about how well the process has worked. This latter method of evaluation has the advantage of being carried out by a member of a peer group but with a more objective perspective.

External reviews have to be handled carefully to ensure that the reviewer or agency has a clear brief and understands the context and culture of the organisation within which they are working. Organisations must give careful consideration to the brief they give reviewers and the scope of the audit they wish them to undertake.

Given the sensitivities that relate to campaigning it may not always be easy to get the candid views of some of the leading participants, particularly if they are civil servants. This can be partly overcome by using the informal feedback gained from meetings with these audiences. Lobby agencies offer audit and strategic planning services for organisations at a price.

On some occasions organisations find that there are other agencies in the area which are able to provide follow-up work from which they can make an evaluation. The Ramblers' Association was fortunate in that the Countryside Commission re-surveyed the question of rights of access to farmland after the Association had carried out a major campaign. This allowed it to monitor the impact of the campaign and it was able to conclude that, while the ploughing-up of footpaths was still a problem, it was less so than it had been.

Such reviews are often most useful when an organisation needs to have a broader view of its activities or where the trustees or directors feel that internal plans are not working or need changing but there is no consensus on how to move forward. These types of review are often used as a lever of change within the organisation.

DIFFERING PERSPECTIVES

There may often be a number of different perspectives and expectations held by an organisation and its stakeholders and different parts of an organisation will have differing perceptions. All these may need to be taken into account in campaign evaluations. For example, beneficiaries may concentrate on the outcomes of the campaign in terms of immediate changes to legislation and policy, while for fundraising staff the most important aim may be raising the profile of the organisation. While clarity about overall objectives is important, evaluators also need to be sensitive to the different perspectives and pressures within an organisation.

THE USE OF SURVEYS IN EVALUATION

There are divergent views on the usefulness social survey techniques when evaluating campaigns. In many cases there is no obvious target for the survey.

Questionnaire design, distribution and analysis all take time and resources. There is also a likelihood of a very low response rate unless there is an exceptionally strong motivation for the respondents. Nevertheless, there are occasions when the use of such techniques can be justified and produces useful results. It is often beneficial, at the end of a campaign, to survey at least some of the more involved participants. They are in a position to give valuable feedback about what they thought of the campaign material and the other briefings and campaign actions they were involved in. They can also be asked to make suggestions for future campaigns.

The survey format needs to be kept extremely simple to ensure a good response rate and ease of analysis. Such surveys can also be especially useful if the organisation is campaigning internationally and there is little possibility of meeting with campaign memberships or other parts of the organisation face to face. Amnesty International received a high response rate to a member survey it carried out to evaluate a campaign on women's rights. The organisation was then able to make changes to its campaign techniques that reflected the concerns of regional campaigners.

A key question is always, Who is the evaluation for? In writing an evaluation report it is always important to keep in mind the various audiences that may have an interest in it and make sure that the recommendations are relevant for them. Trustees are more likely to be interested in the relation between the outcome of the campaign and the original objectives, as well as in the reasons why some objectives may not have been achieved. They are also likely to take an interest in the resources which were spent on the campaign and the responses from its various audiences. Campaign staff will need to know in more detail how particular procedures worked in delivering results and the members may need feedback on the outcomes but not the process of the campaign.

THE ROLE OF TRUSTEES IN EVALUATION

Trustees have a responsibility under the guidelines on campaigning issued by the Charity Commission to ensure that campaigning activities constitute an efficient and effective use of the charity's resources in pursing its objectives (see Part 2 and 10). This responsibility is discharged in a number of different ways within the charities studied for this guide. In many smaller organisations, in addition to their role on the board, the trustees are often engaged in leadership roles in relation to political activities and therefore are fully informed about the way a campaign is going. This is often the case in small organisations like Families Need Fathers, where there is very close contact between the campaign staff and the management committee or board. Larger organisations have much more formal systems for keeping Trustees informed. Regular reports may be produced for the board on current campaign activities and major policy decisions adopted only after formal consideration by the board. Whatever the system, a clear process for reporting and agreeing campaigning objectives must be established so that trustees can be clear about what they are committing the organisation to and so that the organisation can act as a single body.

The last point is especially important for organisations where only a limited number of trustees are involved with a campaign and the rest of the board are involved only in decisions such as agreeing policy and evaluating results. If there are no proper reporting procedures, there is a danger that the board can become isolated from the activities of the organisation at large. It may be particularly difficult for board members of smaller organisations where trustees are heavily involved in campaign activities, to maintain objectivity about a campaign. In these cases it may be particularly appropriate to ensure that the evaluation mechanisms in place chart the success of campaign activities from a more detached viewpoint.

By establishing relationships through which trustees, staff and volunteers learn about each other and about their environment, organisations can enrich their working culture and expand their expertise. By doing so, they are more likely to achieve their aims. The role of trustees in campaigning is further explored elsewher in the guide.

Good campaigning organisations will constantly wish to improve their work. Evaluation is the vital process whereby organisations can learn and apply those lessons to the next campaign. Many organisations will neither want nor be able to adopt all of the ideas outlined in this chapter. However, the more that these working practices are integrated into a general approach, the easier the task of evaluation will become.

Part 4.
Keep it Legal!

10.

'Charities in England and Wales have a long and distinguished history of contributing to social reform. They continue to make an invaluable contribution to issues central to the well-being of the community today'.

'By the very nature of their knowledge and social concern…some charities are well placed to play a part in public debate on important issues of the day and to make an important contribution to the development of public policy. Others will invariably be drawn into such debate'.

(Charity Commission, Political Activities and Campaigning by Charities CC9)

A number of myths have grown up around what political activities are permissible under charity law. This is largely due to the only available guidance being somewhat confusing and contradictory. However, the clarifications introduced by the Charity Commission's guidelines on political activity have defined the boundaries of political activity in a helpful way. As long as charities stay within the Commission's guidelines, they are able to pursue political activity, and a number have already done so with considerable success. Indeed, charity campaigning has continued and grown as the law has developed. Furthermore, many campaigners regard the most recent changes to the Commission's guidelines as a step forward in defining best practice.

NEW GUIDELINES FOR ACTIVE CHARITIES

The new guidelines, *Political Activities and Campaigning by Charities* (Charity Commission, CC9), were issued by the Charity Commission following extensive consultation with the charity sector. They endeavoured to clarify the Commission's interpretation of the law as it relates to the political activities of charities. The guidelines apply to registered charities only and do not affect other voluntary or not-for-profit organisations.

The main regulatory framework depends on case-law judgements and the Charity Commission's interpretation of these. There is a perception that the Commission is critical of political activity and that it undertakes a large volume of investigations but this is not the case. In fact the guidelines support many of the political activities that charities currently undertake. There are over 180,000 registered charities in the UK and only a small proportion of these are investigated in any year. Of the 247 cases in 1994 where the cause for concern was substantiated:

19 (66%): were concerned with maladministration;
43 (14%): revealed evidence of deliberate malpractice;
 5 (2%): identified improper political activities.
 3 (1%): were concerned with tax abuse;

(Source: NCVO)

The vast majority of cases are resolved by organisations being advised to amend their course of action or make corrections to campaign materials in the future. No cases have been recorded where trustees have been asked to repay the funds spent on campaigns. However, the mere existence in the guidelines of the term 'impermissible political activities' is often enough to make trustees nervous, and sometimes over-cautious, about what activities they can legitimately undertake.

CHARITABLE OBJECTS

All activities that charities carry out should be seen to further their charitable objects. The objects of a charity are set out in its governing documents — a constitution, trust deed or the memorandum and articles of association — and define the underlying purpose of the organisation. It is important that a clear statement of the charity's purpose can be derived which relates to those objects. Many charities also have 'mission statements' which relate these objects to a simple statement summarising the purpose or goal of the organisation. Mission statements, by clarifying the purpose of an organisation, are useful in establishing what political aims lie within its purposes. Organisations must ensure that, in the production of a mission statement, they do not go beyond the limits defined by their objects. It is always the objects that will be the final arbiter of the power trustees have to authorise action in respect of political activity.

SAMPLE MISSION STATEMENTS

BARNARDOS
Working together to challenge disadvantage and create opportunity.

WWF (WORLD WIDE FUND FOR NATURE)
To achieve the conservation of nature and ecological processes by:

- preserving the diversity of genetic species and eco systems;
- ensuring that the use of renewable natural resources is sustainable now and in the longer term for the benefit of all life on earth;
- promoting actions to reduce to a minimum pollution and the wasteful exploitation and consumption of resources and energy.

OBJECTS VERSUS ACTIVITIES

The guidelines make it clear that the objects of charities cannot be mainly political; the primary purpose of a charity cannot be the furtherance of a change in legislation or government policy. However, political activities designed to further a charity's objects can be undertaken if they can be shown to be ancillary to the objects and appropriate to the charity's overall activities. As the Charity Commission's document puts it:

'Charities must not be political organisations. But they are not precluded from all political activity. A distinction must be made between political purposes and political activities. The Courts have made it clear that a body whose stated purposes include the attainment of a political purpose cannot be charitable. A body whose purposes are charitable may nevertheless engage in activities which are directed at securing, or opposing, changes in the law or in government policy or decisions, whether in this country or abroad.'

The distinction between activities and purposes is based on case law, most notably what has become known as 'the Amnesty International Case' (McGovern v. Attorney General [1982]), in which Justice Slade concluded that a trust for political purposes can never be regarded as being for the public benefit and hence could not be considered as being charitable. Such trusts include those set up to:

- further the interests of a political party;
- procure changes in the laws of a country;
- bring about the reversal of government policy or decisions.

If the objects of a trust are charitable, however, then the trustees have incidental powers to employ political means in the furtherance of their objectives without depriving the trust of its charitable status.

Organisations such as Amnesty International, Liberty and Friends of the Earth are not, under these rules, charitable organisations. Some organisations have sought to bypass the restrictions by setting up separate campaigning arms to the parent organisation, such as War on Want Campaigns. However, most organisations that wish to carry out activities without restraint from the guidelines have not sought charity registration but have created separate bodies to carry out research and associated educational activities. The Commission does not look favourably on registering charity subsidiaries created solely to avoid the restrictions imposed by the guidelines.

THE ROLE OF TRUSTEES

Trustees need to keep in mind these distinctions when applying for charity registration and or considering campaign activity. Political activities may be undertaken as long as it is clear that they are in the furtherance of the aims and objectives of the charity. Trustees have the primary responsibility for ensuring that an organisation's campaigning activities are within the boundaries set by its purposes and that they adhere to the law relating to political campaigning. If trustees cannot demonstrate a clear relationship between the activity undertaken and the benefit to the group or issue named in the organisation's objectives then they stepping beyond the limits of their powers as trustees.

> 'To be ancillary, activities must serve and be subordinate to the charity's purposes. They cannot, therefore, be undertaken as an end in themselves and must not be allowed to dominate the activities which the charity undertakes to carry out its charitable purposes directly'.
>
> (Charity Commission, CC9: para.9)

The trustees' role is crucial in ensuring that the balance of resources devoted to the achievement of an organisation's purposes by political means is in line with the requirement that such activity be ancillary to the main purpose of the charity. This may be judged by the resources that a charity gives to its campaign activities in relation to the other means by which it achieves its objectives. Clearly, if the expenditure on campaign activities exceeds that devoted to an organisation's other activities then it would be difficult to regard campaigning as ancillary. This does not mean, however, that a charity must attempt to give the work it does relating, for example, to service provision a higher *public* profile than its campaigning activity.

> 'The trustees must be able to show that there is a reasonable expectation that the activities will further the purposes of the charity, and so benefit its beneficiaries, to an extent justified by the resources devoted to those activities'.
>
> (Charity Commission, CC9: para.9)

This stipulation may feel challenging for trustees and staff in its insistence on the importance of having clear plans which identify the potential benefits should an activity succeed. It forces trustees and staff to take a close look at the aims and objectives of campaigns to ensure that, within the bounds of best practice, the actions an organisation takes can be justified in terms of the outcomes achieved. It is not enough to simply believe that the activity will be beneficial. This is not to say that only those activities which trustees are sure will lead to successful campaign outcomes can be pursued but only that they must reasonably expect that, if successful, the campaign will achieve its target and further the purposes of the charity.

Given the crucial role that charity law assigns to trustees, it is important to be clear about who constitutes the governing body of a charity and what is their role. Ultimately, responsibility for the political activities of the charity must be discharged by those trustees responsible under the charity's governing document for controlling the management and administration, regardless of what they are called (Charity Commission, CC3). This group may have different names such as management committee, council of management, or board.

Voluntary organisations can benefit greatly if trustees and staff are encouraged to work closely together. However, both parties must understand their own and each others' roles and the functions of governance and management must be sensitively performed. Trustees working with staff, must seek to contribute their expertise and experience and oversee the work of the organisation rather than interfere with it.

The trustees can develop ways of working with campaign staff that allow them to have closer contact with the operational aspects of an organisation. This does not absolve them from approving the overall direction of a campaign, the level of resources it has available and making key policy decisions. In considering these issues they also have to judge whether the activities undertaken will further the interests of the beneficiaries and are an effective use of the charity's resources. The board is also responsible for ensuring that the appropriate tone and style are maintained in the campaign.

Involving Trustees in Campaigning

The level of trustee involvement will vary from one organisation to another. In the organisations surveyed for this guide this was achieved by:

- direct reporting by campaigners to the board on a regular basis;
- establishing formats for reporting campaigning activities with criteria set by the board;
- creating a sub-committee of the board with devolved responsibility for campaign issues;
- developing procedures for approving campaign reports and materials;
- ensuring the involvement of the board in campaigning actions;
- holding a special session of the board to consider the campaign strategies for the year as part of the strategic plan of the organisation;
- nominating a trustee to have special responsibility for campaign activity.

The organisations which responded to *The Good Campaigns Guide* survey had a wide range of relationships with their trustees. These depended in part on the type of organisation but there appeared to be no simple correlation between charitable and non-charitable status and relationships with trustees.

The Carers National Association has a federal structure with the board elected by the members. While day-to-day management decisions are made by staff, policy decisions are approved by the board of trustees. Trustees play a supportive role in relation to campaign activity and they help to set corporate direction and strategy. The Royal Society for the Prevention of Cruelty to Animals (RSPCA) has a sub-committee of the full RSPCA Council which is responsible for ultimate decisions about which campaigns go ahead and what resources are devoted to each campaign. The Council plays a crucial role in the assessment of different campaign priorities in an organisation which may have upwards of 200 campaigns at any one time.

At Greenpeace, which is not a charity, the role of trustees in campaigning activity is limited. As Doug Parr puts it:

> As far as I know, the trustees have no role in the process [of planning campaigns]. The board has a very strategic role, which means that it does not interfere in operational matters, which are exclusively the responsibility of the Executive Director and Senior Management Team...the trustees have an even lower role in the process — so low in fact I don't even think I could tell you what it is!

At the other end of the spectrum, Stonewall, another non-charity, has developed a different role for its board. Palmer explains it in these terms:

> The group are in effect shareholders, and a similar number of them, six or seven, are invited to become the Board of Directors. The board's role is the most hands on...the group's is to provide direction. For example, their latest request is 'we'd rather you campaigned for partnership rights than for marriage rights'. The group makes decisions about the issues rather than the means...the board works closely with the management team in setting priorities.

Organisations need to think clearly about their board structure and the most appropriate way in which trustees can monitor and be involved in campaigning activities. *The Good Campaigns Guide* survey suggested a number of good practice ways this could be achieved and Figure 15 illustrates a number of devices which have been designed to ensure proper trustee scrutiny of and involvement in campaign activities.

All these activities are part of the means by which trustees can gain a full understanding of the political activities in which they are engaged and, therefore, be in a position to understand the evidence they are presented and make informed judgements.

Figure 15 Activity/ Campaign	**Formal requirements** Reporting mechanism	**Informal (good practice)** Other forms of involvement
Generation of proposals	• The board or sub-groups kept involved in campaign thinking, awareness of changes to the environment affecting the objects of the charity. Briefing on government proposals and thinking on responses to them.	• Lead trustees kept informed of developments. Sub-groups that advise and work together with campaign staff on general issues. • Specific task groups to look at particular issues.
Policy decisions	• Reports to the board generally via senior management. • Policy decisions taken by trustees with advice from campaign and management staff. • Agree allocation of resources through the budget cycle or other appropriate means.	• Working party or sub-group of the board where policy issues can be discussed and reactions of trustees to proposals gauged. • Trustees take responsibility for different campaign areas or interests.
Planning	• Relevant plans presented to the board for approval.	• Informal consultation with staff and members on campaign ideas, timetable, and content. • Planning group from campaign staff with nominated trustee involvement.
Communication	• Regular reports to trustees on ongoing campaign activity including changes to original plans. • Clearance procedure for policy documents, reports and other sensitive materials or communi- cations, i.e. press releases likely to raise issues in relation to the guidelines or the law	• Regular meeting of trustees, staff and members to discuss issues, be briefed on new reports and campaigns. • Membership briefings and newsletters. • Learning forums, open meetings to seek member's views.
Evaluation	• Results of campaign activity with analysis of outcomes and plans for future activities.	• Focus group of those involved in the campaign to review progress. • Trustees involved as part of the evaluation process.

11.

The guidelines are the Commission's interpretation of the current state of the law. The Commission has considerable powers and can investigate a charity that it judges to have broken the guidelines. The Commission responds to complaints rather than proactively investigating charities. The first stage of the process is a letter to the charity raising the issue of concern. If the complaint cannot be satisfactorily resolved, the Commission has the power to launch an investigation as it did in the case of Oxfam (Charity Commission, 1991), and make recommendations or instruct a charity to alter its behaviour. It has the power to call for papers and publish reports, and to hold trustees personally liable for expenditure on campaigns that could not be justified by reference to the objects of the charity, though this power has rarely been exercised. The Commission can also make recommendations on restricting the future political activity of a charity.

DEALING WITH POLITICAL PARTIES

> 'A charity must not support a political party.'
>
> (Charity Commission, CC9: para.40)

A balance must be maintained between a charity's dealings with all the different political parties. This does not mean that they must be treated equally in the sense that any campaign communication or invitations to meetings must be circulated to all political parties. It is perfectly legitimate for campaigners to pursue particular issues with ministers without having to brief the opposition. However, as a matter of courtesy and good practice, organisations would do well to keep all parties aware of their concerns on an equal basis. This does not mean that when arranging public meetings organisations must attempt to achieve a balanced platform. Party conference meetings are an obvious example where this simply would not be possible. However, it is important, over the range of its activities, that an organisation can show that there has not been a bias in respect of any political party.

> *'A charity should not seek to organise public opinion to support or oppose a political party which advocates a particular policy favoured or opposed by the charity. It is inevitable that sometimes a policy put forward by a charity coincides with that of a particular political party.'*
>
> (Charity Commission, CC9: para.18)

As part of the aim of campaigning is to influence the policies and practice of decision makers, it would be surprising if the views of political parties and charities did not converge at times. Charities must still ensure that their views do not simply echo a political party's position and hence promote the policy of that party in a partisan way. Charities may publish the way MPs have voted on a particular issue but particular care not to seam biased should be taken during an election because of the obvious political sensitivities of such a period (see the section concerning electoral law below).

CAMPAIGNING, EMOTION AND ARGUMENT

> *'Except where the nature of the medium being employed makes it impracticable to set out the basis of the charity's position, a charity must not seek to influence government or public opinion on the basis of material which is merely emotive.'*
>
> (Charity Commission, CC9: para.30)

> *'Provided all other requirements are met, material produced in support of a campaign may have emotional content'.*
>
> (Charity Commission, CC9: para.20)

> *'They [the trustees] may publish the advice or views they express to Ministers. They may also seek to inform and educate the public on particular issues which are relevant to the charity and its purposes, including information about their experience of the needs met in their field of activities and the solutions they advocate. But they must do so on the basis of a reasoned case and their views must be expressed with a proper sense of proportion.'*
>
> (Charity Commission, CC9: para.10)

In the overcrowded arena of public debate, with many issues vying for attention, it is the aim of a good campaign move its target audience. More often than not campaigners are constrained by the medium and are not able to express all the points of an argument. It is therefore important that what they do put out is well-reasoned and factually based. The emotive content of the campaign should not mislead the public. The Commission's guidelines respond to the suspicion that such techniques are exploitative, gaining the weight of public opinion by the use of simplified arguments. Emotion must not be used as a substitute for sound argument.

The Commission's concern reflects the difficulty of coming to terms with the changing landscape of political campaigning. While campaigning does need to be based on sound argument, it could be said that the Charity Commission's view of the political process ignores the necessity for campaign groups to demonstrate public support for the case they are putting if they are to attract the attention of decision makers. This area of the guidelines remains the one that is likely to cause continued difficulties of interpretation and controversy.

INFORMING THE PUBLIC

'A charity must not invite its supporters, or the public, to take action in support of its position without providing them with sufficient information to enable them to decide whether to give their support and to take the action requested'.

(Charity Commission, CC9: para.31)

If a charity wishes to engage public opinion, sufficient information must be presented to allow the public to make an informed judgement about the case being put to them. This requirement is often used by the Commission in assessing how far claims are merely emotive, i.e. lacking in the appropriate supporting evidence for the argument being advanced.

ACCURACY OF INFORMATION

'A charity must not base any attempt to influence public opinion or to put pressure on the government, whether directly or indirectly through supporters or members of the public, to legislate or adopt a particular policy, on data which it knows (or ought to know) is inaccurate or on a distorted selection of data in respect of a preconceived position'.

(Charity Commission, CC9: para.27)

An organisation is expected to check the provenance and accuracy of all the data it uses and it is responsible for that data. It would not be a defence to suggest that it did not know that something was inaccurate. An organisation must take reasonable steps to ensure that all evidence is validated. If it is found out, subsequently, that a campaign used invalid data, it would normally be enough for an organisation to issue a correction and apology unless it could be shown that the organisation should have been aware of the failings of its data. The general principle – that information should be accurate – is indisputable and forms the bedrock of successful campaigning. The cost to an organisation's reputation if it gets its case wrong or is seen to provide misleading information can be devastating. It may take years to build back the confidence of an MP or the public if an organisation is seen to have got its facts wrong.

DEMONSTRATIONS AND DIRECT ACTION

'A charity must not participate in party political demonstrations'.
(Charity Commission, CC9: para.28)

It is not only party political demonstrations that may cause problems for charities. The Commission has specific concerns about the nature of demonstrations and direct action and has issued an annexe to the guidelines to deal with this issue.

If organising a campaign event or demonstration, charities remain within the guidelines if the event involves them in no more than the provision of information in the form of a reasoned argument, such as handing out leaflets in a public place. However, different considerations apply if the event moves beyond this type of activity. A charity can only organise or take part in rallies, demonstrations and speeches if they form part of a well-founded and properly argued campaign, which, when seen as a whole, satisfies the requirements for campaigning outlined earlier in this chapter.

The Commission recognises that public events offer charities significant opportunities to publicise their position. However, it fears that if charities participate in events that go beyond what is merely educative or informative, the public will regard their activities as inappropriate. The more campaigning activity moves away from reasoned argument, the more the Commission fears it will interfere with the rights of others. There are also concerns that, should a demonstration or rally dissolve into public disorder, charities risk incurring civil or criminal liability and attracting adverse publicity. The Commission's view is, therefore, that charities must think extremely carefully before taking part in any demonstration. Restrictions are also placed on demonstrations by The Public Order Act 1986 and the Criminal Justice Act 1995 (see below).

Charities must ensure that, if they are involved in demonstrations, they take appropriate precautions to prevent their members from placing the organisation in breach of the guidelines. These precautions could include the provision of:

- clear guidance on the law in this area;
- a full briefing of the issues the demonstration is seeking to publicise;
- stewards to ensure that the demonstration proceeds in the way planned by the organisation and supporters can be given guidance and support throughout.

Demonstrations are high-risk activities for charities because of the potential lack of control over participants. However, it is unlikely that the Commission would hold a charity to account for the actions of demonstrators who have no association with the charity, as long as it has taken reasonable steps to comply with the guidelines.

CHARITIES AND RESEARCH

'A charity which conducts research must ensure that it is properly conducted using a methodology appropriate to the subject'. (Charity Commission, CC9: para.50)

Good campaigning should always be backed up by evidence relating to the issue at hand. Detailed knowledge of the circumstances of beneficiaries gives charities their moral authority and establishes the veracity of their case.

The process of managing research breaks down into a number of stages:

- identifying the issue
- defining the research brief
- commissioning the research
- agreeing the methodology
- carrying out the research
- reporting and disseminating the results

The Commission is particularly sensitive about research in a political context because of the dangers of it being used in a partial or partisan way.

Charities currently use a number of methods when carrying out research:

- employing dedicated research staff within the charity;
- commissioning independent research companies or educational institutions;
- using the above methods but with sponsorship from a third party;
- using volunteers, members or supporters of the charity;
- funding a separate institution to carry out research which is published by a separate body.

With all these methods the 'public benefit' criteria applies. The trustees must satisfy themselves that the scope of the research falls within its objectives and is for the public benefit. In practice, this means that it enhances the charity's knowledge of its issues and be of use in furthering its aims through the dissemination of information to the public. It is unlikely, therefore, that research undertaken primarily for commercial gain would be treated as valid charitable activity. Under charity law, charities also have an obligation to publish or use the results of any research they conduct.

It may be difficult for trustees to exercise judgement over technical issues relating to the research methodology such as the implications of complex medical findings. It would therefore be prudent for them either to avail themselves of professional advice from within their own organisation or make reference to external advice from suitably qualified experts. Many organisations proceed by a mixture of these methods.

Trustees must also evaluate the way the research is carried out. This will include making an assessment of:

- the expertise and appropriateness of those carrying out the research;
- the quality of the research proposal and the likelihood of it achieving its stated aims;
- the appropriateness of the methodology to those aims;
- the balance between the level of funding and the outcomes that the research promises.

Again, the trustees can discharge these responsibilities by taking the advice of expert internal and external advisers. However, it would not be good practice for those proposing the research to also be the ones judging its appropriateness.

RESEARCH AND ETHICS

Trustees also have to consider the ethical implications of any research project. This is a complex area which includes the use of human volunteers in research, the use of animals for medical research and the complexities of researching disadvantaged or disempowered groups while respecting their dignity. Research inevitably raises these issues. The key question for trustees is whether they have mechanisms in place to explore the implications for the charity and whether the research protocols conform with the charity's overall aims and the wishes of its beneficiaries. Internal guidelines and procedures must be developed to ensure that the trustees have the opportunity to debate any issues involved and their implication for the charity's position.

CAMPAIGNING IN ALLIANCES

> 'A charity may affiliate to a campaigning alliance even if the alliance includes non-charitable organisations'.
>
> (Charity Commission, CC9: para.41)

Charities frequently find themselves in circumstances where they can make a better use of time and resources if they campaign as part of an alliance. Alliances also make it possible for charities to gain greater impact and a broader base of support. However, individual organisations need to be clear about their objectives in joining a campaign alliance. A charity should only affiliate if there is a reasonable expectation that by doing so it will be furthering its own charitable purposes. It must also make sure that it does not undertake activities through the alliance that it could not undertake in its own right.

One of the main problems of campaigning in alliances is that decisions may need to be taken during the course of a campaign without there being an immediate means of consulting with all the alliance members. While the Charity Commission guidelines recognise that this may create problems for a charity, they are clear that, as soon as the charity is aware of activities undertaken by the alliance that go beyond what is permissible under the guidelines, then it must disassociate itself from those actions and ensure that any funds given to the alliance are not used for those purposes. A charity cannot use affiliation to a campaigning alliance to fund a campaign that could not be undertaken in the charity's own right.

ACCOUNTABILITY FOR LOCAL AND REGIONAL CHARITIES

Local charities are uniquely placed to assess and represent the needs of their communities. They have detailed knowledge of the special circumstances affecting the life of those communities and a commitment to advance the interests of people they serve in those localities. They are well placed to play a key role in the public debate about the future of those communities both through local decision-making bodies and their MPs.

The Commission is issuing guidelines for charities who operate at the community level which are similar to the guidelines for national charities but which take account of issues relating the size and position of local charities.

Charities with integral regional or branch structures need to rationalise the lines of accountability between the national body and local branches. While this is relatively straightforward for charities with clear regional structures there are a number of charities that have membership or affiliation structures that are more complex. These can include:

- A charity with a number of regional branches or groups but where there is only one charity registration and board of trustees. There may be local committees but the national trustees are responsible for all activities at the national and the local level.
- Autonomous local charities: These will be registered as charities in their own right and have a separate charity number. They may well affiliate to the national body.
- A mixture of the two arrangements, with some charities having local groups under the parent body's registration number, and larger groups becoming independent with their own charitable status.

If an organisation has local groups that use its charity name or membership structure, then it is also liable for their activities. It is, therefore, vital to establish accountability between national and local branches. Mechanisms to approve and communicate policy are of critical importance. Organisations should use policy forums and annual general meetings to set policy lines and priorities. Engaging the hearts and minds of local groups is essential to establish the legitimacy of the campaign and to secure the cooperation of the membership. Local groups need to be kept informed about the progress of campaigns and any adjustments made to the claims and information being produced by the national body.

In serious cases of disagreement or instances when a local group exceeds the parameters set by the national body, the national organisation must consider what sanctions it has available, including withdrawal of the charity's name in extreme circumstances. Ideally charities should set up model agreements with local groups detailing what can be expected by both sides of the partnership.

When a local charity is a separate entity then its own trustees are responsible for the actions of that charity even if it participates in a campaign run by the national body to which it is affiliated.

CAMPAIGNING FOR COMMUNITY CHARITIES

Community charities are subject to the same rules as national bodies. Clearly, the kind of campaigns possible and the ways in which campaigning is conducted depends to a large degree on the size of the charity and the resources it has at hand. Nevertheless, whatever the campaign strategy, trustees and staff must operate within the bounds set by the Charity Commission. Charities would be well advised to ensure that, after discussion by trustees, the decision to mount a campaign is formally recorded. Issues that trustees should take into account in mounting a campaign should include:

- the objectives of the campaign;
- the benefits of the campaign for the beneficiaries;
- which staff or trustees are authorised to represent the organisation during the campaign;
- the budget for the campaign;
- a process for evaluating what has been achieved.

These processes obviously have to be adjusted to the size of the organisation and could be drawn up in a fairly simple document. The process could also serve as a useful way of clarifying for staff and trustees what they are trying to achieve. Local campaigns often challenge local authority decisions on the allocation of resources or service delivery; such activities generally fall well within the guidelines. As with national bodies, local charities can seek to influence the views of MPs and local councillors and has the right to publish the way representatives have voted. They must be careful to use this only to exert public pressure upon the office holder.

There are a number of areas where local charities can engage in political activities by:

- inviting MPs and councillors to public meetings in order to comment upon party activities which relate to the purposes of the charity, subject to the constraints of electoral law;
- publishing MPs' and councillors' views in newsletters – as long as a representative range of views are published. If it is not possible to present a balanced argument, then a clear indication should be given of the reasons why;
- publishing advertisements for political parties in charity publications, on proper commercial terms, for the purpose of raising funds. In doing this, charities must not discriminate between political parties unless there is a specific way in which the activities of a particular party might conflict with the charity's purposes. For example, an organisation set up to further the aim of promoting racial harmony might be justified in refusing advertising from a party that promotes the virtue of racial difference, however, see the following chapter on electoral law;
- contacting MPs and councillors and seeking their support in issues relating to the way the charity is funded and in matters concerning grant applications or disputes over resource allocation.

The situation will often arise when members of a local charity board have been assigned by the local authority. When acting in the capacity of trustee, these representatives must not use their position to forward the interests of a political party or the authority that they represent. Further guidance is given on this by the Charity Commission (Charity Commission CC29, 1996).

12.

Other Laws and Regulations

A FRAMEWORK FOR GUIDANCE

The Commission's guidelines exist within a general framework of charity law, electoral law and standards and codes of practice that relate to public order, advertising and the rights of petition. To understand the legal context to campaigning it is useful to examine all these areas.

KEEPING ON THE RIGHT SIDE OF THE ADVERTISING STANDARDS AUTHORITY

Advertising in non-broadcast media is governed by the British Code of Advertising Practice. This code covers the content of press, posters, direct mail, cinema and any other form of non-broadcast advertisement. The code is supervised by the independent Advertising Standards Authority to ensure that it operates in the interests of the public. Its remit is to ensure that advertisements are 'legal, decent, honest and truthful'. Investigations are activated via complaints from the public. The Authority has the power to investigate complaints and make rulings. While these are not legally binding, the sanctions on advertising agencies that produce and place the advertising are serious and include the publication of the Authority's ruling in the case concerned. Advertising agencies only get recognition from the Authority if they accept the code; to be seen to be flouting it is considered a serious matter.

In 1993, the code was amended to include issues relating to public policy. The Authorities reach now extends to advertisements placed by charities, pressure groups, trade unions, and commercial bodies. Advertisers must be able to substantiate any claims they make in an advertisement. There must be evidence to support any factual claims made and the claims should be truthful in the general impression that is created by the advertisement. Political parties are *not* covered by these requirements.

The simplest way to get a feel for the way the authority operates the rules is to look at the complaints it upholds and those it rejects. Here are two examples:

ASSOCIATION OF LONDON AUTHORITIES

The first takes the form of a complaint to the Advertising Standards Authority about a poster from Association of London Authorities which claimed 'Every year 100,000 women in London seek medical help because of domestic violence...'

The complaint was upheld by the ASA because:

> *The advertisers explained that the figure had been taken from a television documentary but failed to submit adequate documentation to show that the figure was accurate. The Authority therefore requested that the figure be deleted from future advertisements until such time as it could be fully substantiated.*
>
> (ASA Monthly Report, No.39)

INTERNATIONAL FUND FOR ANIMAL WELFARE

Tesco and some members of the public complained about an International Fund for Animal Welfare (IFAW) national press advertisement which showed a man about to club a seal and had a caption blaming Tesco's Chairman and other British supermarkets because they sold Canadian fish. The complaint focused on the link made between harvesting salmon and seal killing and the offence caused to Tesco's Chairman. The Authority supported all complaints against the IFAW, ruling that it used misleading information, and stated its disapproval of the link made with Tesco's Chairman. (ASA Monthly Report: No.57)

Conversely, the Authority turned down a complaint from the Canadian Sealers Association which objected to national press advertisements run by IFAW. The advertisements claimed that 10,000 seals were killed annually so that their penises could be sold to the Chinese, and implied that the Canadian Government was involved in a cover-up. On this occasion, the Authority ruled in favour of the IFAW as it had supporting evidence on both counts. (ASA Monthly Report: No.57)

The Authority tends to be fairly liberal in the way it interprets the code, especially in comparison with the controls that apply to the broadcast media. The independent broadcasting industry is regulated by the Independent Television Commission and the Radio Authority and governed by the regulations of the 1990 Broadcasting Act.

Political advertising by pressure groups is banned under the 1990 Act. The Act's powers were challenged by Amnesty International following the Radio Authority's outlawing of an advertising campaign about atrocities in Rwanda in May 1994, but the challenge was rejected by the courts. The regulations have also prevented the Red Cross running a television campaign about the dangers of land mines which was to have been screened on MTV.

At the time of going to print, a Green Paper was in circulation incorporating proposals from the European Commission to harmonise marketing rules throughout the European Union. This would be more liberal than the current regulations and the Green Paper specifically identifies the existing ban as being disproportionately restrictive.

Television advertising has not yet attracted attention from campaigners largely due to the prohibitive cost. However, there are restrictions, most notably that advertisements from charities must 'handle with care and discretion matters likely to arouse strong emotions in the audience' and 'avoid presenting an exaggerated impression of the scale or nature of the social problem to which the work of the charity is addressed' (ITC Code of Advertising Standards and Practice: Rule 10).

The general requirements are very similar to those that appear in the Charity Commission guidelines on the use of emotive arguments and advertising.

LIBEL LAW

The law of libel should be taken seriously by campaign groups. The potential costs of a libel suit could be disastrous. The anti-fur campaigning group Lynx went into liquidation in 1993 following a successful action by a mink farmer disputing Lynx's allegations that mink were kept in unsuitable conditions.

Defamation is split into two categories: slander, which is spoken, and libel, which is written. *Libel* extends to cover statements that have a lasting impression, such as those made on television or radio, while slander *reserved for what are regarded as* more transitory statements with no lasting effect. The latter is judged mainly by whether the plaintiff can prove that there has been financial loss. Libel is about the damage that a statement does to someone's reputation. Simply saying something that is untrue will not necessarily constitute an insistence of libel unless it is also damaging to their reputation. The defence against an allegation of libel is to show that the statement made was true. It will also help to show that the opinion was honestly derived and that there was no malicious intent – in short, that the defendant was not 'acting with reckless disregard for the truth'. In both cases the burden of proof rests with the party that made the original statement. It is possible for someone to be sued even if the libel they have committed is unintentional. In this case, defendants must be able to show that reasonable care was taken in publication and an offer of apology or retraction was swiftly made.

ELECTORAL LAW

Organisations thinking of campaigning during the period of an election or seeking to raise the profile of an issue need to ensure that they do not breach the rules laid down in section 75 of the Representation of the People Act 1983. This prescribes strict limits on the use of expenses by candidates. It states:

> 'No expenses shall, with the view to promoting or procuring the election of a candidate at an election, be incurred by any other person other than the candidate, his election agent and persons authorised in writing by the election agent on account:
> (a) of holding public meetings, organising public display; or
> (b) of issuing advertisements, circulars or publications; or
> (c) of otherwise presenting to the electors that candidate or his views of the extent or nature of backing or disparaging another candidate'.

The expenditure of candidates has to be strictly accounted for during elections and must stay within the limit set for all the candidates. All expenses which relate to the promotion of a candidate's views to the public must be paid from the election allowance. This is to ensure that no candidate has an advantage because of third-party sponsorship. Failure to comply with the Act could leave the candidate or the organisation open to criminal prosecution and fines of up to £2,000 or six months' imprisonment. If such a case is heard in the Crown Court, the maximum sentence is 12 months.

Section 110 of the 1983 Act also requires that the publisher of any material during an election is clearly identified in any material that makes reference to the election. The organisation responsible for the material would in this case count as the 'publisher'.

PROMOTING OR PROCURING A CANDIDATE

The main thrust of electoral law in this area, therefore, is the restraint of expenditure. Activities which do not involve spending money are largely unaffected by electoral law. However, activities which do involve financial expenditure are prohibited if they are conducted with the intention of promoting one candidate or party. For example, an organisation could not produce leaflets during an election which urged people to vote for a particular candidate. Equally, organisations cannot urge people not to vote for a particular candidate, as to do so would have the effect of promoting the collective chances of all the other candidates and would therefore breach section 75 of the Act.

It also breaks charity law to seek to persuade members of the public to vote for or against a candidate or for or against a particular party. While charity law is not applicable to non-charitable voluntary organisations, it is highly unlikely that the constitution of any such organisations would allow them to 'promote or procure the election' of a particular candidate.

APPROACHING INDIVIDUAL CANDIDATES

Voluntary organisations are permitted to visit or write to candidates setting out their specific concerns and asking candidates for their own opinions on those concerns. The Charity Commission guidelines state that a charity may bring to the attention of prospective candidates issues relating to the purposes of the charity, or the way in which it is able to carry out its work, and to raise public awareness about the organisation generally, provided that the promotional material is educational, informative, reasoned and well-founded.

PRESS COVERAGE

There are no restrictions under electoral or charity law for voluntary organisations seeking press coverage of their concerns during the period of an election provided that insodoing they do not breach the general principles of both charity and electoral law as set out above.

USE OF PERIODICALS

Voluntary organisations can continue to use publications to promote their concerns during the course of an election provided such publications appear as part of a regular, periodical schedule and are not specially produced for the election. Any proposed election edition should not be so out of keeping with the usual style and content of a periodical as to constitute a different publication altogether.

HOLDING A PUBLIC MEETING

Opinion is divided as to how far voluntary organisations are free to organise public meetings during an election campaign. In addition to facing requirements regarding balance and the endorsement of candidates' views, voluntary organisations are also restricted by financial considerations.

Under section 75 of the Representation of the People Act, any money used for public meetings must be accounted for. Expenses incurred must be included in candidates' returns of election expenses.

Figure 16: The law and Campaigning

Activity	Check by:	Governed by:	Relevant legislation and law:
Research	• Review of research procedures. • Peer Review		• Charity Commission guidelines CC9 • Law of libel (i.e. Defamation Act 1952)
Non-broadcast	• Advertising Standards Authority advise on copy, usually within 24 hours	• British Code of Advertising Practice	• Law of libel
Television	• The Broadcast Advertising Clearance Centre clear for the ITC code at script and finished version. Advertising Agencies will automatically send to the BACC,	• The ITC Code of Advertising Standards and Practice	• Broadcasting Act 1990 • Law of libel
Radio	• See above	• The Radio Authority Code of Advertising Standards and Practice	• Broadcasting Act 1990 • Law of libel
Cinema	• Advice avaialble at script stage from the British Board of Film Classification.	• Certification required by the British Board of Film Classification	• Law of libel

News releases	• Charity Commission will advise on the suitability of materials in relation to the guidelines.	• Charity Commission guidelines CC9	• Law of libel
Campaign materials	• Charity Commission will advise the suitability of materials in relation to the guidelines. • Check with legal advisors if concerned about the possibility of libel action.	• Charity Commission guidelines CC9	• Law of libel
Parliamentary lobbying	• Sergeant at Arms' Office, House of Commons. • Metropolitan Police if related to a demonstration.	• Charity Commission guidelines CC9	• Public Order Act 1986 • Criminal Justice Act 1995
Demonstration	• Local authorities and the police.	• Charity Commission guidelines CC9	• Public Order Act 1986 • Criminal Justice Act 1995
Public meetings — private premises	• Local authorities and the police.	• Charity Commission guidelines CC9	• Public meetings Act 1908 • Representation of the People Act 1983
Public meetings — public places	• Local authorities and the police.	• Charity Commission guidelines CC9	• Public Order Act 1986 • Representation of the Peoples Act 1983 • Local Acts of Parliament • Criminal Justice Act 1995

Accordingly, some sources of advice suggest that voluntary organisations are free to call public meetings during the period of an election if, prior to staging such meetings, related costs are covered by one or more of the invited election candidates and accounted for as part of their election expenses. In effect, a voluntary organisation cannot convene a public meeting without prior authorisation from the candidates prepared to bear the expenses.

However, advice given by the Home Office during the course of the 1997 general election suggests that the costs of holding public meetings during an election period do not necessarily constitute an election expense and voluntary organisations are therefore free to organise such meetings. It must be stressed, however, that opinions differ on this issue and campaigners should seek legal advice before taking any action.

In any case, an organisation arranging a public meeting during an election would be well advised to invite candidates from all political parties. Voluntary organisations cannot afford to imply by their actions that they prefer some candidates or parties to others. All invited candidates must be given an equal opportunity to speak. If, however, one or more of the candidates fail to appear, the meeting can still go ahead, although it is advisable for campaigners to offer to read a statement from the absent candidates and make clear that they were invited.

Voluntary organisations should not use public meetings as an opportunity to endorse a particular candidate's view. Members of the public attending the meeting should be free to come to their own conclusions. The hosting organisation should, therefore, not seek to sum up the views of the candidates nor present an opinion of its own which can be held up in comparison to that of any of the candidates.

The major concern of electoral law is to ensure that the candidates' election expenses are not supplemented by donations or the financing of activities that they would otherwise have had to pay for themselves. It is not intended to prevent organisations raising legitimate questions during an election period and participating in the political process. Campaigning organisations must purge their campaigning materials of any language that could be seen as supporting the views of one candidate. The period during an election is regarded as particularly sensitive and charities still need to have regard for the Charity Commission's guidelines. Indeed, this area is so fraught with potential danger it may be advisable for all campaigning organisations to consult with legal advisers to be sure they stay within the limits of the law.

SOCIETY FOR THE PROTECTION OF UNBORN CHILDREN

In September 1996, the European Commission on Human Rights ruled that, during the course of the 1992 UK general election, the Society for the Protection of Unborn Children had been within their rights to distribute leaflets which set

Figure 17

Illustrates the process of campaign development prescribed by the law, the charity guidelines and the media codes of practice.

Identify Issue	Ensure that the campaign meets with the purposes and objects of the charity.
↓	
Research Issue	Ensure that the research is done to an acceptable standard as defined by the guidelines. Ensure that facts are checked — also check for emotive use of material. Check legal opinion if necessary.
↓	
Produce Campaign Materials	Ensure the campaign falls within Charity Commission guidelines objectivity and check that campaign does not support one political party.
↓	
Launch Campaign	Check the relevant permissions have been acquired for any demonstration. Ensure that supporters who are going to be using materials are well briefed on the campaign facts.
↓	
Campaign Events	Check that relevant permissions have been acquired for any events. Ensure that supporters are briefed about the law relating to demonstrations. Brief stewards and provide summaries of the campaign case.
↓	
Media Work	Check statements to ensure that they are not libellous. Ensure that claims made can be backed up by evidence. Make trustees aware of theclaims claims you will be making. Ensure an appropriate tone and and style are used.
↓	
Lobbying Parliament	Ensure that your approach is not party political. Send communications to any relevant members with an interest and ensure that you stay within the Nolan Report's recommendations in relation to MP's conduct.
↓	
Advertising	Ensure that relevant clearances are obtained.

out the views of the candidates on abortion. This decision overturned the Representation of the People Act which prohibits organisations spending money to inform the electorate as to candidates' views on issues. However, decisions of the European Commission must be endorsed by the European Court and, at the time of printing, the Court had yet to make its judgement on this issue. If the European Court does give its endorsement, the UK Government will be required to remove some of the restrictions contained in the 1983 Act.

KEY LEGAL AREAS OF CONCERN

What follows is not an exhaustive list but a guide to the main areas of legislation or guidance that apply to campaigning activities.

Figure 17 illustrates the process of campaign development prescribed by the law, the charity guidelines and the media codes of practice.

IN CONCLUSION

While the requirements discussed in this chapter may seem onerous many are grounded in good campaign practice and others are the basic requirements of the law. Adherence to these rules will not only ensure that campaigners do not fall foul of the law but that campaigns uphold many of the principles that inform effective campaigning. If these practices are ingrained in the everyday procedures and working methods of organisations in the voluntary sector, the less they will seem like external constraints and the more likely they are to become common working practice.

Part 5

The Changing Face of Campaigning

13.

'...the vitality of a democracy, the vitality really even of a market system, is very much dependent on the existence of this kind of organisation that exists outside of the state, that exists outside of the market, and through which individuals are free to exercise their right to work together for common purposes.'
    Dr Lester Salmon, Director of the Institute of Policy Studies, John Hopkins University

'One who adapts his policy to the times prospers, and likewise the one whose policy clashes with the demands of the times does not.'
    Machiavelli, The Prince

Campaigning is going to be profoundly affected by the changes to political and mass culture that are now taking place. The growth of the voluntary sector has already challenged the institutional and legal framework leading to a spate of recent reports ending with the Deakin Commission Report on the Future of the Voluntary Sector (NCVO, 1996). However, as the role has developed, so has the complexity of the environment in which voluntary sector campaigning takes place.

If campaigning groups want to retain and expand their role, they need to take account of these changes and be able to respond to them.

The development of campaigning is influenced in four key areas:

- the crisis in political legitimacy of the government and political parties;
- the role of pressure-group politics in democracy;
- the political and financial independence of charities;
- the impact of new methods of communication.

THE CRISIS OF GOVERNMENT AND POLITICAL LEGITIMACY

Government has always played the role of arbiter between a number of different interests, expediently managing these and the electorate's expectations in line with its own policy agenda. Pressure groups have often acted as mediators between government and the public, to the benefit of both.

However, the relationship of government to both the public and pressure groups is changing. Public perception of politics and politicians is on a downward spiral. While this has led to a growth of involvement in pressure-group activities, cynicism about the legitimacy of political activity, together with an imbalance between elected and non-elected forms of representation, has led to a crisis within the more traditional forms of political representation. The growth of the quango state has added to the confusion about where accountability now lies within the political system. The success of single-issue pressure groups has led to increasing scrutiny of their tactics, their legitimacy and the effect they have upon democracy.

During the years of the Thatcher government, there was a reversal in the consultative nature of the political system, a process not substantially altered under John Major (Baggot, 1995). The loss of influence with government has led to a decline in the power of many interest and sectional groups, such as trade unions, and some sectors of the business lobby. However, during this period, many single-issue and charity groups have expanded. The influence of some groups within the system has remained steady or grown, especially that of to civil servants. This trend is particularly evident in relation to the specialist areas that concern many charity and voluntary groups. The change has taken place against the background of a sometimes hostile policy environment and increasingly constrained public finance regime.

The continued dependence of some government departments on the expertise and local knowledge that pressure groups can bring has also meant a continued and often enhanced role for many such organisations. Thus, pressure groups have used their influence, within a policy framework mainly dictated by the government, to maintain influence within their sphere of interest. In the cultivation of their own policy communities, government departments have used and often co-operated with pressure groups to get outcomes that are amenable to the department and to the pressure group. It is unlikely that that this trend will disappear since the issues that government has to deal with get more complex and its need for the support and advice of interest groups who act as intermediaries between itself and various publics increases.

With the new Labour government it will be interesting to note if its attempts to work more cross departmentally and to reflect more peoples priorities have an input.

A Crisis of Legitimacy?

'It is the right of everyone to lobby Parliament and ministers.'

(Lord Nolan, 1995)

The growth in campaigning has also given rise to a renewed interest in – and public sensitivity to – the methods and objectives of campaigners. The public is becoming suspicious of the techniques used by many lobbying agencies to influence decision makers. An ICM poll for *The Guardian* showed that 42 per cent of those voters polled thought that the activities of lobbying agencies harmed democracy, with only 8 per cent thinking that they helped the working of democracy (*The Guardian*, 8 October 1996). The reports of the House of Commons Select Committee on Members' Interests and the Nolan Committee Report have led to increasing cynicism about the openness of the political system and the honesty of politicians.

Desire to protect the democratic process from inappropriate influence has also led the European Parliament to adopt a report at its plenary session on 19 July 1996 which sets out a clear framework for lobbying activities. The aim of the report is to ensure that decision making is transparent and that Members of the European Parliament can take decisions without being subjected to undue influence from outside interests. The author of the report argues that the European Parliament should not be 'a supermarket where those with the biggest pocket can buy what they like. Members have a responsibility to engage in dialogue with lobbyists, whoever they are. But dialogue must not turn into ownership' (Ford, 1996).

Interestingly, Ford's report highlights the problem that voluntary sector and community groups have of gaining equal access to the European Parliament because of the resource issues involved for such organisations. This suggests that there is a need to facilitate the lobbying work of voluntary sector bodies and provide equal opportunities for organisations representing the interests of civil society.

Charities have escaped much of the public scrutiny turned on other campaigning organisations. However, there is no reason to believe that the press or public will make any distinctions between the work of charity-sector campaigners and that of the commercial sector unless the charities maintain the highest professional standards. In this climate, charities and pressure groups must be able to justify the methods they use and the place they hold in the political community. It is important, therefore, for campaigners to ensure that the time and resources spent on campaigning are used effectively and that supporters are comfortable with the style and tone of the campaigns undertaken. With public cynicism about the morals of politicians, these measures are essential for a sector that wants to claim the moral high ground.

UNACCOUNTABLE AGENCIES

The role of campaign groups has been complicated by the development of non-governmental agencies. The devolution of executive powers to 'next steps' agencies, the revamping of local authority functions, the arrival of urban development corporations, the creation of new ways of organising health services through health trusts and commissioning agencies, and the development of Training and Enterprise Councils have dramatically changed the map of national and local government in the UK.

New 'next steps' agencies now control £60 billion of government expenditure in ways that are less accountable to the state or citizens, while local authorities now have less control over many of the services they provide and rely on the government for 85 per cent of their funding (Hull and Weir, 1996). Many of the old forms of representation and political participation no longer seem legitimate. This 'democratic deficit', the lack of parliamentary or other forms of local control over many areas of public life or finance, combined with a loss of faith in traditional forms of political activity, has created a new role for pressure groups. It is through these groups that much displaced civic concern is now channelled and this may represent the birth of a different kind of politics.

The implications for campaigners are profound. The ability to exercise democratic control through Parliament has undoubtedly diminished. Getting information about the operating performance and targets of Training and Enterprise Councils, to take one example, has been extremely difficult because of their status as private companies. Parliamentary scrutiny is deflected in the name of commercial confidentiality, yet the devolution of operational accountability to a different level has created a huge number of posts on the boards of these quangos. There has been concern about who gets appointed to these positions and why, but a more open recruitment policy, possibly as a consequence of the Nolan review, could open up the prospect of more accountable local structures and representation on many of the management boards of these organisations at community level.

Also, some of these boards have made efforts to inform themselves and ensure community representation. These structures offer their own potential for democratic accountability but they are not built on the traditional forms of accountability that the sector has been used to under local government. A major challenge for local action remains how to hold these organisations to account. However, there is some measure of devolved responsibility from central government, albeit within a centralised financial regime, which suggests that there is scope for amending their role and their level of accountability to the community. It will be up to the sector to find ways of coming to terms with these changes and using these to reinforce democracy at a local level so that the views of members and users can be represented and their needs taken into account.

A LANDSCAPE OF POLITICAL DISILLUSIONMENT

There has also been a decline in the confidence placed in government's ability to produce workable legislation. This is reflected in the views of business on the competence of government legislation. Thus 70 per cent of a panel of a 100 opinion leaders though that overall the quality of legislation over the last decade had declined (Opinion Leader Research Survey, April 1994). The public shows a growing mistrust of the political system and the competence of politicians.

Opinion polls of the electorate reflect a profound sense of disillusionment with the ability of the government to represent their views. A poll by ICM for Channel Four News found that 71 per cent of 1,427 adults, interviewed in March 1994, agreed with the statement, 'The voting system produces governments which do not represent the views of most ordinary people'. The public's faith in Parliament is also at an all-time low. Whereas in a 1973 survey half of those polled thought the British system of government worked well, by 1995 three-quarters of respondents thought that the system should be improved (Dunleavy and Weir, 1995). Research for the Rowntree Trust by MORI also found that while, in 1991, 58 per cent of the public believed that Parliament worked 'fairly well', this figure had fallen to 43 per cent by 1995 (Dunleavy and Weir, 1995). This was confirmed by research carried out by The Henley Centre and NCVO. In response to a question asking if they had a great deal or quite a lot of confidence in parliament, 54% answered yes in 1983 but this has fallen to 10% in 1996. (Henley Centre/NCVO 1997). The crisis of political representation has been one of the major driving forces behind the development of single-issue campaigns and pressure groups.

Also political activity, at least as currently practised by the major political parties, offers few attractions to those wanting to express a moral concern. In a study by Michael Argyle, on the sources of happiness, people ranked political activity as the lowest contributing factors yet involvement in charities was the placed second highest (cited in Mulgan and Landry, 1995: 20).

Voluntary sector and pressure group campaigning has tapped into this desire for other forms of involvement. It now plays an important role in retaining and

Figure 16:
Membership of environmental organisations
(in thousands)

	1971	1994
Friends of the Earth	1	112
National Trust	278	2,152
Ramblers' Association	22	100
Royal Society for the Protection of Birds	98	870
World Wide Fund for Nature	71	187
Greenpeace	0	300

(Source: Social Trends, 1996)

developing a real sense of the pluralism that is a cornerstone of participatory democracy. Many voluntary organisations who have sought to recruit, support and train their members in campaigning and lobbying skills have found a willing and growing membership. The involvement of members and supporters has brought many sections of the public into a relationship with government at national and local level, but not principally through the old channels of political parties or trade unions.

NEW EXPRESSIONS OF A CIVIC SOCIETY

> *Although party-political activity has declined, for very good reasons, this is not true of political activity at its widest. The agitations against the poll tax or the Criminal Justice Act, or the M11 road builders, or the export of live animals by boat or the Child Support Agency, are examples of a contemporary protest politics that involves huge numbers of citizens, focusing their attention narrowly perhaps, but effectively for all that.*

> (Marr, 1995)

The growth of campaigning and single-issue pressure groups is a feature of an evolving civic culture of participation which mirrors the decline of more traditional forms of political activity. The government recognised and tried to exploit this trend with its active citizenship campaign in the early 1990s but met with little success.

While it would be a mistake to see the composition of voluntary groups as heterogeneous (they represent a huge range of activity and interests), the potential for the voluntary sector to provide an alternative focus for politically active citizenship should not be underestimated. A renewal of civic culture much-touted is taking shape through the development of voluntary sector and charity campaigning and advocacy.

Increasing sensitivity to public opinion and the awareness of influence of organised interests on the government's agenda are features of the current political landscape. Ministers, media managers and civil servants struggle to develop and promote the government's agenda in a complex political environment. Any issue from the transportation of live animals to road policy has the potential to blow up in the government's face.

DIRECT ACTION

This creates dilemmas for campaigners trying to represent their interests effectively and influence the debate: 'How can we combine being part of the establishment — able to lobby Ministers — and yet carry on campaigning for radical change in the way animals are treated?' (Parminter, 1997). One sign of the crisis of legitimacy in traditional forms of political representation has been the growth of various forms of extra-legal protest, such as blockading trucks transporting live animals or tunnelling to prevent new road developments. These forms of campaigning are likely to become even more widely used — and will come to be seen as legitimate forms of protest by growing sections of the public — as long as the current forms of representation and accountability are perceived to be ineffective.

There are question marks, however, over what such forms of protest actually achieve. As Chris Rose, Campaigns Director of Greenpeace, noted in relation to a campaign to stop building the A30 road, 'The road will be built anyway, and raising awareness is no longer enough' (Rose, 1997).

There is often a false dichotomy drawn between direct action and other forms of campaigning. The careful lobbying of decision makers and the drama of direct action are considered by many to be at the opposite ends of the campaigning spectrum. Yet, as can be seen from the case studies in this guide, direct action can be used effectively as part of a well thought out campaign strategy. The crucial issue in campaigning terms is whether direct action is indeed used as a tool within well-planned, strategic campaign or whether it becomes an end in itself.

Campaigners have successfully used many forms of direct action to publicise causes while remaining within the law: vigils have been used outside social services offices to draw attention to the withdrawal of services; the problems of disabled and elderly people have been highlighted by a campaigner dressing up as the Chancellor of the Exchequer and sitting in a bath outside the Treasury; peaceful demonstrations have been held outside foreign embassies to draw attention to the plight of political prisoners. All such actions have been taken as part of the unified approach of planned campaigns.

What type of action is taken and how aggressive it appears are important considerations. Clearly, organisations charitable can not be associated with actions that are outside the law. However all organisations need to consider carefully not only the legality of direct-action campaigns but also the impact they are likely to have on public opinion.

Furthermore, campaigners who seek to capture attention for their causes through direct action must also find a means of holding and sustaining the public's interest and must consider whether their use of direct action merely signals their lack of power and their inability to influence the course of events through legitimate means.

DEMOCRACY AND THE ROLE OF THE PRESSURE GROUP

The role that campaigning and voluntary groups are taking in this new political environment is beginning to change the fabric of decision making in government and business. Pressure-group politics can offer citizens the chance to exert influence in areas where Parliament has been perceived to fail.

Pressure-group politics cannot balance one social good against many others, but it does allow for a broader variety of views to enter the public arena and leaves politicians with the task of balancing the various interests. However, the role of pressure groups has been questioned because of the fear that they could undermine the democratic process. Campaigning groups have been characterised as representing only narrow interests and, if such interests are allowed to dominate, executive decisions will be made for the benefit of special-interest groups at the expense of a silent majority. This is already seen as a particular problem at local level where the expertise of many middle-class protesters has led to successful campaigns against various 'undesirable' local developments. Even if the not-in-my-back-yard ('NIMBY') campaigns are removed from this equation, there are legitimate concerns that it is the articulate and relatively well-off groups that will dominate local and national political agendas.

Conflicts have also emerged between local authority members, who are elected to serve an area, and local voluntary organisations, often representing large sections of the community. As Andrew Marr has observed in his study of developments in the state of democratic government in the UK, these conflicts have become fairly common as the new politics rubs up against established structures:

> There is growing and irrefutable evidence of the rise of a new kind of community politics in Britain the political parties are only vaguely involved or not involved. The array of self-help groups, community schools, neighbourhood schemes, voluntary organisations and devolved local authorities that have started to criss-cross housing estates, boroughs and villages are beyond the imagination of Westminster local campaigning organisations, all of them meaning more to many middle- and working-class communities than traditional politics has realised. (Marr, 1995:100-1)

However, voluntary bodies, regardless of their weight within the local community, can claim no legitimacy for their views beyond that which is accorded to the case they present. Politicians, as the elected representatives of the community, have the duty to strike a balance among the different interests within the community. Furthermore, campaigning groups must look to their own internal standards of democracy if they wish to make claims about representing the interests of the communities they serve.

The role of local authorities has come into question as their power to control local spending and service decisions has declined. In response, local authorities are seeking new ways of safeguarding local democracy through partnerships between different sectors. A renewal of civic leadership at local level could go hand in hand with the continued development of voluntary sector advocacy and campaign groups which give new life to community involvement.

THE QUALITY OF LEGISLATION

Another argument often rehearsed is that pressure groups damage democracy by encouraging the government to legislate quickly in response to the latest public outcry, leading it to produce poor legislation. The most obvious point about this argument is that it confuses the respective roles of the participants. Lobby groups can represent their members' interests, but it is up to the government to make decisions on the basis of the evidence and to produce workable legislation. This does, of course, raise the question of whether undue pressure has been put on the government to make such decisions, which is why transparency and honesty within the political system are so important.

Secondly, there is little evidence that pressure from voluntary sector groups has resulted in unworkable legislation. The most often-cited case is the Dangerous Dogs Act 1991, introduced after public pressure, led by the RSPCA, following some well-publicised cases of pit bull terriers savagely attacking children and adults. The Act led to the registration of 8,500 dogs and the destruction of 430. These measures brought criticism from some dog owners and there was a general perception that the Act was a knee-jerk reaction to public pressure. However, a recent report from the Home Affairs Select Committee, which examined all the evidence available, found that the Act 'has largely succeeded' (*The Guardian*, 19.12.1996).

For pressure groups to be a threat to democracy they would have to have more power than the other forces they are ranged against. Overall, their strength lies in the development and promotion of particular interests and their actions can only be considered to be distorting democracy if all the other pressures upon the executive and Parliament are ignored.

The real issue is not whether voluntary organisations have too much influence, but to what extent their influence is restricted by a policy-making framework that is often constrained by an agenda set by government rather than the voluntary sector, and by public finances that frequently give them very little room for manoeuvre. Pressure groups have much success in achieving results in their particular interest areas which are significant for their beneficiaries, but rarely do they alter the overall thrust of government policy. One such rare instance was the Disability Discrimination Act of 1995. Even here, though, much in the Act went against the then government's deregulatory instincts, and the way in which it was implemented remained a compromise between the campaigners' and the government's views of how the legislation should be framed.

Concerns about the influence of pressure groups on the democratic process are, on the whole, are overstated. It should also be remembered that, although pressure groups do represent particular concerns, they are also legitimate channels of that concern. To the extent that they are able to participate in a dialogue with government, democracy is being served, as long as these dealings are above board and not open to abuse.

It is likely that public involvement in pressure groups will continue to grow as long as disillusion with the old style of party political politics persists. Despite the recent increase in Labour Party membership, the overall trend in political affiliation and party membership has been downwards and, where there are new memberships of political parties, they are substantially different in composition to those that have gone before. Many of the old, local structures of involvement have been abandoned and memberships exist more on a national basis in a similar way to many charity membership schemes.

THE END OF POLITICAL PARTIES?

What may be happening is a convergence of the new style of single-issue activist with a new type of party membership more attuned to the politics of single issues and membership than the old style of political activist. This may make the political arena even more volatile, as old allegiances break up, further blurring the boundary between political party membership and pressure-group campaigners.

The consequence may be that, without a thriving local basis, parties will fail, in the long run, to fulfil the functions that liberal democracies need (Seyd and Whiteley, 1995: 456-472). In the absence or failure of institutions whose role it is to aggregate interests over a broad spectrum, narrow interests can take over, and the most effective of these usually represent the most affluent and powerful, allowing those with most power and resources to be heard. The converse of this however is that strong parties that form strong governments may protect powerful interests which can have the same effect. The challenge for the future is to produce strong democratic structures that go beyond these dichotomies. Single-issue pressure groups are not the cause of the declining credibility of existing political institutions but one of its symptoms.

However it is no use harking back to the old forms of party activism. New models need to emerge from the experience of both styles of political organisation which take account of the vastly changed landscape within which both now operate. 'Civil society' is not an arbitrarily constructed alternative to the state. It is made up of institutions and associations whose powers are defined and regulated by the state and which, in many cases, would not exist without state support. The issue now is to set the right level of regulation and establish new forms of political involvement that encourage the development of a flourishing civic culture.

In relation to campaigning, these aims could be met through the following provisions:

- The voluntary sector needs to ensure that standards of campaigning are professional and open to scrutiny. Only by doing so will it retain the high moral ground it currently occupies.
- Trustees need to be fully involved in campaigning and public advocacy

issues. Training must be provided to ensure that they are able to fulfil this role.

- The sector needs to develop relationships with democratically accountable bodies and explore new forms of participation and accountability with statutory agencies through intermediary bodies that bridge the gap between statutory and non-statutory agencies, as suggested in the Deakin Commission Report on the Future of the Voluntary Sector (NCVO, 1996: 56).
- Statutory agencies and government need to look at how they can facilitate small groups and intermediary bodies to fulfil their representative role, as noted in the Ford Report (Ford, 1996).
- Two central principles for organisations conducting charity campaigning activities should be public accountability and transparency in their dealings with other sectors. The Nolan Committee recommendations on the accountability of public bodies could form the basis of standards in this area (Lord Nolan, 1995).

14.

THREATS TO VOLUNTARY SECTOR CAMPAIGNING

There are a number of possible threats to the role of voluntary sector campaigning in the future. The independence of the sector is vital if it is to continue to fulfil and develop the role it has begun to set out for itself. Two key areas are the legal restraints on charity campaigning and the impact of contracting for services.

CHARITIES AND REGULATION

Charitable campaigning is already more regulated than commercial lobbying and the restraints put on the sector have led to concerns that campaigning by charities is being unreasonably constrained in comparison with other pressure groups in the commercial sector. How far should charities be restricted in relation to their campaigning activities?

Some argue that the restrictions on charity campaigning should be lifted and that the public should be allowed to say, via their donations, if they disagree with the position being taken by those they support. Such competition in the field of ideas, given free reign they hold, would be more healthy and promote the best ideas (Perri 6, 1994).

While the argument for removing all restrictions on charity campaigning is attractive, it ignores many of the features of pressure-group campaigning that make the marketplace for ideas a much less perfect one than the argument presupposes. Not only do all groups not have equal access to the marketplace but it is difficult to see how total deregulation of charity campaigning would improve incentives for those with less of a voice or improve the standing of those within the sector.

Campaigning charities take pains to ensure that they are seen as being free from allegiance to any one political party, and very few see this as a restraint.

The public tend to trust the claims of charities because they are seen as non-partisan and this is one of the major factors attracting supporters of charity campaigning. While deregulation would not automatically lead to the defining of charities' allegiances along party lines, it is likely that there would be pressure from members to politicize. Furthermore, it would create difficulties for supporters who might want to contribute to the general relief work of an agency but not to its campaigning work if that work were allied to a single party.

A major concern for charities is not the ability to express support for the policies of a political party, which is already permitted under the current guidelines, but the restrictions placed on the ways in which they are able to publicise their campaigns. The legal framework needs to evolve beyond the current, overcautious interpretation of case law. There are still many passages within the Charity Commission guidelines that could be improved to bring them into line with current campaign practice without conflicting with the demands of the law.

The challenge is to find a less paternalistic and more open form of charity law which is based on a recognition of contemporary methods of campaigning but which ensures that the practice does not become unduly politicised.

CAMPAIGNING VS SERVICE PROVISION

> *'The voluntary sector is swimming into the mouth of Leviathan'*
> (Frank Prochaska, cited in NCVO News, 1996).

The growth in the voluntary sector's direct provision of services is sometimes looked upon as jeopardizing the sector's advocacy. It has also been suggested that the only solution to this dilemma is for a distinction to be made between the campaigning role of the sector and service provision within the terms of charity law (Knight, 1993). Others have expressed concern that the expansion of government funding has further curtailed the sector's ability to represent the best interests of it clients. While there are undoubtedly potential conflicts between local authorities and service-providing agencies, this argument is founded on a misunderstanding of the general context of charity campaigning. There are a number of factors which make the situation more complex – and the embrace of Leviathan less imminent – than these arguments suggest:

1. Charities rely on a mixture of statutory funding and public money raised by donation. The fundraising capability of these organisations guarantees a level of independence from the influence of central or local government by providing the means to pursue their agenda without depending on contracts from any source. Campaigning is paid for in this way, not through contracted work.
2. Even where organisations have substantial government funding they are able to resist government pressure because of their public profile and the position

of moral authority. The Refugee Council and Shelter, for example, have each maintained a publicly critical stance towards certain government policies while receiving funding from government grants and contracts.

3. There is no clear division between service provision, advocacy and campaigning. The provision of services gives many organisations a strong link to those they represent. It is often by functioning as service providers that organisations are able to identify gaps or inadequacies in those services and this can add to an organisation's credibility as a representative to government and others. The voice of such organisations would be incomparably weaker if they isolated their service provision functions from their campaigning arms. Furthermore, many of the services developed by these organisations have answered hitherto unmet community needs and function as a form of advocacy achieved via service provision.

4. Charities have the organisational capacity to ensure that potential conflicts between service provision and campaigning are contained and managed. Many organisations maintain a level of formal separation between their campaign departments and service providers. This is not to say that organisational imperatives will not impinge across the two areas but there is little evidence that the sector has substantially altered its advocacy and campaigning functions simply because of the emerging contract culture.

5. It would appear, from a survey conducted in 1995, that the move towards service contracting has not resulted in any reduction of the campaigning or advocacy activities of charities (Richardson, 1995).

As outlined earlier, the imperatives governing the campaigning stance of a charity are a complex mixture of the demands of charity law, the history and positioning of an organisation, the wishes of its members and the scope of its activities. The contracting relationship is only one of the determinants of the public positioning of a charity with regard to campaigning. The charity's overall position and purpose will be as significant as the financial relationship it has with some of its funding bodies.

Evidence from the first comprehensive study of voluntary sector funding shows that grants from statutory agencies and government have not decreased with the growth in contracting. The study argues against fears that the substantial increase in earned income from government could lead to increasing dependence on government or statutory agencies. Government income is balanced by a significant rise in investment income, in grants from other charities and in a continued high level of support from the public. The study suggests, therefore, that the independence of the sector is more secure than had been anticipated (Hems and Passey, 1996).

This is not to deny that there are real dilemmas within campaigning organisations. The relationship between funding agencies and the voluntary sector has become more complicated with the transformation of funding relationships brought about by the change of local authorities to enablers rather than providers. Small voluntary organisations dependent upon a single local authority for funding are more vulnerable to pressure from their funders not to criticise failings in the local provision of services. But even in these cases, local organisations are not without sanctions to impose on funding bodies that try to apply onerous conditions through contract arrangements.

The new partnership that has grown up between local authorities and the voluntary sector has blurred the distinction between statutory and non-statutory provision. A number of intermediary voluntary bodies have developed at local level which voluntary groups can use influence the way local issues are handled. The partnership between statutory and voluntary agencies tends to militate against authorities wishing to muzzle the voluntary agencies which they are also trying to work with. Also, a voluntary agency may be only legitimate body able to deliver particular services. Thus, as with national organisations, there will be a number of influences on local voluntary agencies that will determine their susceptibility to pressure from statutory agencies when considering campaigning and advocacy.

One of the best ways of protecting that local and national agencies are from unwarranted pressure from purchasers is to ensure that such organisations are representative of community and/or user views and can thus be recognised as a legitimate voice and have access to free, non tied or statutory funding.

New Methods for Reaching the Electorate

"There is no one more powerful than a member of a focus Group"
Bill Clinton, President of the United States (quoted in the The Guardian 30.7.97)

Most of the structures of modern democracy predate the methods now available to collect the views and consult with the electorate. The development of new technologies and polling techniques have inspired some democratic writers to propose new ways of involving the public. A range of methods now exist for involving people in decision making, some of which take advantage of new technologies available while others rely on a combination of old and new methods.

Who sets the agenda, how open is the process and how safe the results are from manipulation.

Focus Groups and Opinion Polling

Focus groups and opinion polling have become standard practice for political parties wishing to assess the publicy's reaction to proposals. At best they can be valuable tools for testing out the views of the public on key issues. However, they only measure the views at a particular moment in time and do not allow for those involved to challenge the agenda of those conducting the research. On the other hand, focus groups and opinion polls can offer objective information, when properly conducted.

DELIBERATIVE POLLING™

This method of gauging opinion involves statistically significant numbers of people in an extended discussion leading to a vote or series of votes on an issue. A large number of voters come together to discuss a particular issue in depth via small groups and then in a larger group of up to 300 people. The whole process is normally televised though this is not essential. The main strength of the process is that it allows researchers to monitor opinion over a period of time during which participants get the chance to examine the issue in some depth and be exposed to a number of different viewpoints. The process also allows the organisers to track how far the participants' views change during the course of the process. It corrects the problems associated with the snapshot view of opinion polls while involving a much wider constituency than citizen's juries or other small-scale methods. The organisers control the agenda of the debate but the process is open and not easily manipulated. This method has been used in this country to examine issues as wide ranging as the prevention of crime to the voting intentions of the electorate before the last election. While only commissioned by the media in this country Deliberative Polling sessions have been used in America by a number of statutory authorities. This has involved resolving issues relating to public policy issues as diverse as the sitting of power stations, to the issues surrounding the US primary elections. (Fishkin, James, S, The Voice of The People, Yale University Press, 1997)

CITIZEN'S JURIES ™

The use of citizens juries as a tool of policy formation is on the increase. Such juries are formed of up 16 people recruited as representatives of the community to explore specific policy issues and decide upon options. Citizens' juries have been most developed in Germany and America where they have been used to consider such issues as future energy policy, the care of children at risk and welfare reform. The use of citizen's juries has already become part of the decision making process in some states in Germany, although it has not come to replace the process of democratic accountability. In America, as yet, they have no formal power, but, having attracted considerable media attention, they are beginning to have some impact on the administrative process. In the UK, local government and health agencies are beginning to look at these forums as a way of addressing the perceived failings of local democracy.(Coote, A, Lenaghan, J, Citizens' Juries: Theory into Practice, IPPR, London, 1997)

Citizens' juries allow individuals to scrutinise the evidence and call for witnesses. This permits a high level of control for the participants and facilitates in-depth deliberation. As with deliberative polling, the agenda is set by the organisers yet the results are unmanipulated. The opportunity to deliberate over an issue addresses many of the problems of large-scale polling. However the juries are far less representative of a broad range of opinion and it cannot be presumed that a small set of jurors, exposed to a particular range of information, will make choices representative of the entire community. The analogy with the jury system may also be misleading. Juries are assembled to deliberate on a matter of fact after hearing evidence; citizens juries are typically asked to consider the resolution of competing priorities on the community's resources.

REFERENDA

Referenda can be focused at a local community or used to decide national issues such as whether to join a single European Currency. If the referenda are conducted in an open fashion, then there is the opportunity to consider the main issues. The overall process resembles a national or local election and will share many of the same problems relating to dominance of the media and limited options to challenge and debate the views. However, referenda do offer a chance to hear public opinion and give citizens a real voice over the outcome if the result is binding.

The referendum is going to become an important method for deciding national political issues and possibly local issues. The perceived inability of the existing system to reflect the views of its citizens – coupled with the need to consult on key constitutional issues – will ensure the continued growth of this form of consultation. Different forms of referendum are already used in some American states to gather public opinion and settle issues from gun control to welfare rights. Referenda at national and local level will offer opportunities for campaigners to influence the agendas of decision-makers. Campaign groups will have to plan how to use these opportunities.

TELEVOTE

The televote was developed in America as a means of polling a large number of viewers. Viewers are polled after watching a television show and being sent materials on a particular issue. There have been a number of crude adaptations of this method involving the use of television polling often directly via the television set. Similar polls are often conducted over the telephone after a debate or presentation of a case has been aired on the television. While such an exercise may increase the potential for testing public opinion, the outcome is frequently nothing more than a crude indication of people's views formed by exposure to what is often a dramatic and biased presentation of an issue. They do not allow for those participating to shape the issues or ask questions of the evidence presented.

ELECTRONIC DEMOCRACY

Referenda and polls are increasingly conducted by electronic media, especially in America. Thus polling and voting on issues can be achieved via devices attached to television sets or the telephone. These technique allow for a quick registering of people's views across a wide variety of issues. It is easy to imagine technology that would allow sections of the public to be consulted easily via television, telephone or the Internet. Some writers believe the new technology will bring direct democracy closer to the citizen. (Budge, Ian, The new Challenge of Direct Democracy, Polity Press, Blackwell, Oxford, 1996) However such process leave very little opportunity for those involved to frame the issues and often little time to deliberate on them.

THE FUTURE

There has been concern expressed about these experiments in gathering information. They have been perceived to have the potential to undermine rather than enhance democratic structures by taking the focus away from democratically elected representatives and their mandate. Other critics have referred to the danger of 'government by focus group'. Pointing to the fact that it was Parliament that abolished hanging and legalised consensual homosexual acts against prevailing public opinion, Parliament's role as protecting an enhancing what have at times be unpopular causes or minority rights has been stressed.

These new methods of public consultation, considered alongside the more traditional forms of public meetings, could enrich local national and local democracy: Campaigners need to come to terms with them. It will no longer be enough to focus only on the more formal aspects of the power structure. These new forums will become powerful tools to set national and local agendas in relation to issues such as resource allocation medical ethics. To this extent they could also be powerful tools for campaigners needing to assess the reactions of the public to their ideas. They may also become decisive way to set the agenda for local and national spending decisions and service priorities.

While they offer the prospect of testing public opinion on a wide variety of issues – and therefore offer a powerful aid to decision makers framing policy decisions – there is a danger in using them to absolve politicians and decision makers of their responsibilities to balance complex sets of interests. Such methods cannot replace the complex interaction between public and politicians that sustains national and local government. There is also a danger that many of these methods may not engage the less articulate and those who cannot speak for themselves.

The voluntary sector with its stress on representation and consultation with its beneficiaries is in the position to assist in the development of more varied forms of community representation.

Campaigners need to ensure that proper forms of representation and consultation between voluntary bodies and their members are developed to provide a considered and full representation of members' views.

Government needs to review the formal requirements of accountability on public bodies in order to achieve a balance between the existing financial focus and a more democratic accountability to members and the public.

NEW LABOUR NEW LOBBYING

> "New Labour is a new type of politics"
> (Mandelson, P., Liddle, R., The Blair Revolution, Can New Labour Deliver?, Faber and
> Faber, London 1996)

The new government has set out to adopt a different style and approach from its predecessor. Voluntary organisations interested in campaigning need to consider this change of emphasis if they wish to campaign on a national or regional level. There are a number of elements to the new government's approach which are worth noting.

The Government has placed a great deal of emphasis on seeking to 'renew the trust of the British people in government' as well as looking at rectifying a perceived 'democratic deficit' . In addition, the Government seeks to represent itself as 'being of the people', and not beholden to any special interest group. This produces a new dynamic in the political process. One of the many ways the Labour government aims to go about this task is through direct consultation and polling of the public in order to reach out directly to public opinion. Examples of this include the circulation of millions of leaflets on the National Lottery White Paper seeking comments from the public and setting up of focus group panels to test public opinion. This approach has implications for campaigning by voluntary organisations.

Firstly, voluntary organisations will have to consider how this new approach affects the issues they are concerned with and also consider the clarity and strength of the case they are presenting. With a government that is seeking a more direct relationship with its citizens, voluntary organisations will have to take pains to make a strong case for their causes in order to gain the attention of government, particularly as they will be in competition with other organisations for this attention.

Secondly, the Government's commitment to referendums on key issues of Government policy from devolution to European Monetary Union will bring a new openness and breadth to the way it consults and conducts its business. The referendums will require the mobilisation of support over a number of diverse issues where Government will need to educate and lead public opinion to achieve its goals. The Government is also determined to set the agenda of public debate around its policies by being far more proactive in communicating its policies than previous Governments have been. These developments will lead to a style of communication that will be far more "campaign" orientated and agenda setting. An approach which will have profound implications for campaign groups that have been used to setting the media agenda for Government.

Thirdly, as many voluntary organisations' base their legitimacy on their ability to represent and articulate the views of their beneficiaries/ clients, such organisations will need to be able to demonstrate an understanding of their constituencies' needs. To this end, voluntary organisations must be able to substantiate and effectively communicate the legitimacy of their causes in order not to be bypassed by Government in its eagerness to take a lead on issues which it sees as important."

In addition to wishing to develop a different relationship with its electorate, the Government naturally has its own agenda which; certainly in the short to medium term, has priority. The first few months of the new government, voluntary organisations with interests and client groups which are affected by the Government's agenda have generally received hearings for their cases. However, as the Government wishes to make a virtue out of impartiality, and is determined not to show favours to any sector, voluntary organisations will have to ensure that their arguments and case are well constructed and thought through. Indeed voluntary organisations will need to consider the scope of the government's agenda carefully and see where their interests coincide or diverge and look at the implications of this on their positioning. This will particularly be the case where there are differences in policy.

So far the Government has shown pragmatism in its approach to the delivery of its objectives. It is less concerned with the provenance of the organisations or sectors that it is working with than with their ability to help it further its ends. Good examples of this are the New Deal for Young People which reaches out to employers, voluntary organisations and local authorities. In the case of the reform of the National Lottery, the Government has set out its objectives and invited agencies to come forward with plans as to how these can be achieved. The implication of such an attitude is that the old distinctions between public, private and voluntary sector will start to matter less; the important thing will be to put forward ways of achieving the objectives that the government has set. This pragmatic approach will present many challenges to many long held assumptions about organisational roles.

The tactical decisions about the style of campaigning – whether to mount high profile public campaigns or to use 'insider routes' – will continue to be important one for voluntary organisations. Some organisations that felt they had little to lose by more public campaigning approaches in the past may feel that circumstances have changed, particularly where they are able to receive greater access to discussions with government. However, the familiar dilemma between co-operation and co-option is likely to remain for many organisations, particularly those whose interests may not coincide with the immediate agenda of government. In addition, organisations will have to consider what it means to operate in an environment where the government has a large majority. This has implications not just on direct lobbying of ministers, but also on working with MPs from other parties and with other Parliamentary committees, such as Select Committees.

The Government has indicated that it is seeking strategic partnerships with the different sectors to help deliver its programme and it sees the voluntary sector being very much part of this. This offers voluntary organisations many opportunities, but what is currently unclear is the full nature that these partnerships will take. In the nineteen eighties government looked to the voluntary and independent sectors to take on the delivery of a number of previously state-provided services, particularly in the field of social welfare. It would appear that the current government is unlikely to reverse this trend, but it has indicated that it is looking to redefine the nature of the meaning of partnership. This may have major implications for voluntary organisations, if changes in the format of contracting of services to other forms of partnership arise. It also has potential implications for the scope of campaigning activity. The Government has declared that it intends to seek a 'Compact' with the voluntary sector. The Compact will act as a broad statement of principles unpinning the relationship and is intended to clarify how government will consult the sector and how it will work across government in its relations with voluntary organisations.

The Government has stated its intention to modernise the structure of government and is committed to a process of regionalisation and devolution. The devolution in Scotland and Wales, the creation of regional development agencies in England not to mention the potential creation of elected mayors for London and possibly for other cities are factors likely to have a profound effect on the decision making structures of government. Campaigners will operate in a more diffuse and regionally devolved world. In England, identifying campaign targets will become even more critical with a number of different tiers of decision making between local, regional and national level entering the equation. This will be both a challenge and an opportunity for campaigning organisations. There are likely to be many opportunities for local organisations and national ones with local structures, but new challenges for national organisations without strong regional roots. Regionalisation may also introduce more complexity into a situation where it is already often difficult to identify where decisions are taken and where representations need to be made. For smaller organisations this could exacerbate the current difficulties they have in addressing current power structures.

Overall, bringing power closer to those who are affected by decisions is likely to be welcome to a sector whose values and structures are rooted in local communities. However, the voluntary sector will need to develop its positioning in relation to regionalisation very carefully; currently the sector has very mixed provision of regional infrastructure to support its work. In some regions it has well developed representative organisations, whereas in others such representation is virtually non-existent. The challenge for the sector and indeed for the Government will be to address the support needs and resources of smaller organisations.

The regional restructuring of government goes together with a determination to modernise structure at a national level. This will take a number of forms from changing the procedures of the House of Commons to the possibility of reforming the House of Lords. Proposals to improve the scrutiny of legislation and the strengthening of the role of Select Committees (and indeed reforms to the hours of Parliament) are likely to provide better opportunities for campaigners to influence legislation. It will also mean that campaigning organisations will have to present powerful and coherent evidence, as this will be open to the same extended scrutiny. Again, this suggests that the style of representation and involvement will have to change. The general aim of making the workings of government more open can only benefit voluntary organisations interested in campaigning. If this is also coupled with a Freedom of Information Act and the incorporation of the European Convention on Human Rights to strengthen citizen's access to information and ability to challenge decisions in the courts then there will have been significant change in the context in which campaigning activity takes place .

CAMPAIGNING ORGANISATIONS MUST ENSURE THAT:

1. The quality of their argument is strong and its content factual;
2. That their case is well-researched and gives a clear indication of how the problem can be solved;
3. They are able to tap the potential of modern communication and consultation methods;
4. They know when best to use different campaign methods and positioning with both governmental structures and the public.

IN CONCLUSION

Many of the issues that engendered the growth of pressure-group politics, especially in the charity sector, are likely to persist. The public's lack of confidence in the state to solve social issues continues and people are looking for different ways, at both community and national level, to find new solutions to their problems although it will be interesting to see how things develop after the Prime Minister's assertion that "we are all in this together". The financial conditions that have brought many social issues to the fore, are likely to persist against a background of increasing expectations and limited ability of state finances to meet them.

The voluntary sector incorporates many organisations with strong links to the community and which represent powerful strands of public opinion. The sector is, thus, in a strong position to develop an approach for the twenty-first century that contributes towards the building of a new polity which addresses the crisis of political legitimacy for government.

Campaigning, in its widest sense, has a crucial role in representing the interests not just of privileged sections of the community but of many who would not otherwise have a voice and whose interests and aspirations are often ignored by the political system. Only by ensuring that its campaigns are carried out to high standards which genuinely involve and reflect the views of its constituents, will the voluntary sector be able to fulfil this role.

Campaigning provides people with the possibility of engaging in community activity in a political system that often fails to value the contribution of individuals. The challenge, as campaigning groups grow, is to ensure that they to do not repeat the mistakes of political parties and lose touch with their constituencies.

Appendix 1: Planning tools

ACTION PLANNING

It is important to have a clearly laid out action plan for any campaign. This involves identifying in detail the tasks that need to be completed, who will do them and when. Everything that needs to be done must be listed and assigned to someone. Deadlines for each task must be set and tasks allocated sequentially in the order in which they need to be done. Some action will be dependant on other aspects of the campaign having already been achieved.

To make a successful plan, campaigners need to keep in mind:

- WHAT is the task that needs to be done?
- WHO is going to take responsibility for getting the task done?
- WHERE should the action take place?
- WHEN does the action take place and what implications does this have for achieving the task?

RESOURCE ANALYSIS

Another important aspect of planning a successful campaign is the preparation of a detailed budget. This should include estimates of the financial costs of the different activities and of the projected income. Income predictions should also take account of any costs incurred *raising* that income. Budgets should also include calculations of people's time as a cost.

SWOT ANALYSIS

This technique, frequently used in planning, examines the internal strengths and weaknesses of an organisation and the external opportunities or threats it faces. Below is a framework for a SWOT analysis.

What are the group's strengths?	**Strengths** are positive factors within the group that might strengths? mean you can make an effective contribution to a campaign. Strengths might include: financial material resources, members' skills and time, access to facilities, a good public image, efficient organisational structure, contacts (for example, in the media, or in other organisations), supports, specialist knowledge, language skills, etc.
What are the weaknesses of the group?	**Weaknesses** are negative factors within the group that inhibit your ability to act generally or on particular issues. Weaknesses might include: a lack of experienced members, limited (or no) funds, lack of facilities, poor organisational capacity, etc. It is very important to identify your wekanesses so that you can either take steps to overcome them, or avoid activities that you will be unable to cope with.
What opportunities exist in the wider community?	**Opportunities** are factors about the community within which you work which might complement your group's activities. Opportunities might include: an open and sympathetic press, potential donors, other organisations that might be interested in particular issues or that might be able to put effective pressure on the targets of your campaigning (e.g. trade unions, women's groups, professional groups, ethnic groups, and so on), or links between your community and a country targeted in your campaigning. Again, when planning your work on a campaign or action, consider how you might take advantage of opportunities in your community. For example, if you are planning your work on a campaign on women, and there is a women's group at the local church, that could represent an opportunity to get people from outside your group involved in your campaigning work, and maybe attract donations, new members and make useful contacts for the future. Other groups or individuals in your community are often particularly important in a group's campaigning work, as they may be more effective 'messenger' for appeals to or other forms of pressure on the targets of a compaign/action than your group itself. For example, if the target of a campaign is areligious figure appeals from religious figures in your country may be more effective than appeals from your group members.
What threats exist in your local community?	**Threats** are factors in the wider community that may have a negative impact on your ability to contribute to a campaign or action, or to function as a group generally. Threats will usually be out of our control, although as a campaigning organisation we may, in the longer term, hope to bring about a change in at least some of the factors that represent a threat to our work. Threats might include: political or economic crisis, lack of public interest in human rights issues or in partiuclar concenrs, an intolerance of campaigning or voluntary organisations, a poor image arising from factors beyond the group's control, human rights violations, security issues, local restrictions on our work, and so on.

(Source: Amnesty International Campaign Pack for Local Groups)

ENVIRONMENTAL ANALYSIS — PEST

	Organisation's Factors	Impact	potential response
Political			
Economic			
Social			
Technical			

PEST analysis provides a simple way to order an assessment of the environment in which an organisation operates. Like SWOT analysis it is a useful device for ordering thoughts or inspiring a brain-storming session. It is not a particularly scientific method!

In relation to each area, it is important to consider:

- How important is the influence?
- Is the trend becoming established or is it just a short-term effect?
- Can any changes be predicted in the developments that will mean they are more or less relevant?

Other factors to consider include:

POLITICAL

- changes in government or government policy;
- changes in local authority control, boundaries or policies;
- changes in minister of a department or reorganisation of a department;
- attitude of decision makers to the issue being addressed;
- planned legislation or policy changes to your area;
- changes in European policy;
- changes in membership of key committees or statutory bodies.

ECONOMIC

- impact of the Budget;
- impact of spending plans of government departments;
- impact of the grant allocations from local government;
- impact of the local authority's budget setting;
- state of the national or local economy and its impact on issues such as taxation rates, government spending, etc.;
- company profitability and the effect this could have on business actions.

Social

- expectations about level of services;
- assumptions about improving quality of life;
- changing patterns of social interaction;
- spending patterns, rates of home ownership;
- available leisure time, indices of social concern about various issues.

Technological

- developments in communications technology, the Internet, etc;
- changes in technologies used by companies and the impact this could have on the environment;
- changes to medical science that could affect treatment for particular disabilities or medical conditions;
- new inventions or technologies that alter impact upon the campaign, i.e. new technology for reducing toxic emissions from motor cars.

Appendix 2: Organisations interviewed

Below is a list of the organisations and personnel who took part in structured interviews carried out between September and December 1996:

Organisation	Interviewee
Amnesty International United Kingdom	Rob Beasley Campaigns Co-ordinator
Carers National Association (CNA)	Francine Bates Head of Public Affairs
Families Need Fathers	Trevor Berry President
Greenpeace	Doug Parr Campaigns Director
The Ramblers' Association	John Trevelyan Deputy Director
RSPCA	Kate Parminter Head of Public Affairs, and Alex Ross Parliamentary Officer
Shelter	Tim Hunter Campaigns Manager
Stonewall	Anya Palmer Director
Transport 2000 (T2000)	Stephen Joseph Director

WWF (World Wide Fund for Nature) case study was based on discussions with Michele Corrado, Director, MORI Social Research Institute, UK, and a paper by Michele Corrado and Richard Webber, Head of Planning and Monitoring, WWF International.

We also received evidence for case studies from Mike Parkinson at Oxfam, Adrian Penrose, Campaign Manager for *RSPB*, Janet Titley, Campaign Manager for *Age Concern* and John Trampleasure, Director of Marketing for *Shelter*.

Some of the ideas in the guide were first explored with a group of campaign managers, co-ordinated by NCVO, who meet regularly to discuss issues related to campaigning and charity regulation.

THE GOOD CAMPAIGNS GUIDE QUESTIONNAIRE

GENERAL

Name :
Job title :
Name of organisation :
Address :
Telephone :
Fax :

1. Organisational status (circle one)
   Registered charity/Registered charity with campaigning arm/Pressure group

BACKGROUND

2. What is your organisation's overall mission?

3. What proportion of your organisation's work is campaigning and how does it sit within the organisation as a whole?
   For example, how many staff out of total, how many resources, etc., are devoted to campaigning?

4. What are your main types of campaigning activities?

5. What ongoing alliances does the organisation have with other groups/bodies?

6. How do you monitor and control your campaigning?

7. Who needs to approve campaign decisions and do you have formal internal policy?

8. What role do the trustees have, if any, in this process?

CASE STUDY

Campaign :
Dates :

9. Briefly, what was the issue you built your campaign around?

10. What was the outcome you wanted?

11. Who was ypur campaign aiming to influence and what did you want them to do?
    For example, changing public attitudes/behaviour; changing parliamentary legislation; precipitating direct action, etc.

PLANNING

12. Did you start off with a plan for the campaign?

13. Who were your target audience?

14. What outputs did you want to generate?

15. What activities did you undertake to reach the audiences and achieve the outputs?

16. How, if at all, did you involve your members in these activities?

17. Who were your allies and who were your enemies, both inside and outside the voluntary sector?

STYLE OF CAMPAIGN

18. What were the main messages and what methods did you use to get them across during the campaign?
    For example, emotive of factual; advertising and public awareness or behind the scenes lobbying or direct action; if a mix of tactics was used, what were the most effective?

19. How did you deal with developments that affected the campaign?

20. Did developments make you formally change your strategy?

21. How did you affect these changes?

EVALUATION

22. Did the campaign actually end?

23. Was the end of the campaign announced or did you decide internally to end it?

24. Did the campaign achieve its objectives?

25. What impact did it have, in terms of media coverage, changes in attitudes or support gained from new sources?

26. How as this impact monitored or measured?

27. In terms of the outcome, did you succeed in achieving the outcome you wanted?

28. What other benefits did you get from the campaign?
    For example, raised profile, new supporters, new friends and alliances.

29. How well did your campaign keep up with developments, and how well did you react to changes outside your control?

30. Was any formal evaluation of the campaign done?

31. What lessons did you learn from the campaign, in terms of strategy, planning and evaluation, and how will you change things for a future campaign?

Appendix 3: Advisory Bodies

Action with Communities in Rural
England
Somerford Court
Somerford Road
Cirencester
Glos GL7 1TW
01285-653477

Advertising Standards Authority
Brook House
Torrington Place
London WC1E 7HW
0171-580 5555

British Board of Film Classification
3 Soho Square
London W1V 5DG
0171-439 7961

Broadcast Advertising Clearance Centre
200 Grays Inn Road
London WC1X 8HF
0171-843 8265

Directory of Social Change
24 Stephenson Way
London NW1 2DP
0171-209 4949

Electoral Reform Society
6 Chancel Street
London SE1 0UU
0171-928 1622

House of Commons
Sergeant at Arms Office
London SW1A 0AA
0171-219 3083

Independent Television Commission
33 Foley Street
London W1P 7LB
0171-255 3000

Institute of Charity Fundraising Managers
Market Towers
1 Nine Elms Lane
London SW8 5NQ
0171-627 3436

Institute of Public Relations
The Old Trading House
15 Northburgh Street
London EC1V 0PR
0171-253 5151

The Market Research Society
15 Northburgh Street
London EC1V 0AH
0171-490 4911

The Radio Authority
Holbrook House
14 Great Queen Street
London WC2 5DG
0171-430 2742

National Council for Voluntary
Organisations (NCVO)
Regent's Wharf
8 All Saints Street
London N1 9RL
Tel: 0171-713 6161
Fax: 0171-713 6300
European Officer: lobbying in Europe.
Legal Team: the law and political
activities.
Parliamentary Officer: parliamentary
procedure and lobbying at Westminster.
Social and Public Policy team: developing
good practice in campaigning.
Trustee Services Unit: TRUSTEE
HELPLINE 0171-833 1818,
9.30am-5.30pm, Monday to Friday, and
until 6.45pm on Wednesdays.

The Charity Commission
St. Alban's House
57-60 Haymarket
London SW1Y 4QX
0171-210 4477
2nd Floor, 20 Kings Parade
Queen's Dock
Liverpool L3 4DQ
0151-703 1500

Woodfield House
Tangier
Taunton
Somerset TA1 4BL
01823-345000

Local and community organisations
should contact their national
network, community council or local
council for voluntary service:

National Association of Councils for
    Voluntary Service
Arundel Court
177 Arundel Street
Sheffield S1 2N

Appendix 4: Bibliography

Bachrach, P. and M. S. Baratz, 'Two Faces of Power' in *American Political Science Review*, 1966, Vol.56, pp.947-52.

Baggot, Rob, 'The Measurement of Change in Pressure Group Politics' in *Talking Politics*, 1992, Autumn 5:1.

Baggot, Rob, 'From Confrontation to Consultation? Pressure Group Relations from Thatcher to Major' in *Parliamentary Affairs*, 1995, Vol.48, No.3, July.

Bruce, Brendan, *Images of Power*. London: Kogan Page, 1992.

Charity Commission, *Oxfam: Report of an Inquiry Submitted to the Charity Commissioners*. London : HMSO, 1991.

Charity Commission, CC3, *Responsibilities of Charity Trustees*.

Charity Commission, CC9, *Political Activities and Campaigning by Charities*.

Charity Commission CC9A, Political Activities and Campaigning by Local Community Charities, 1997.

Cobb, Robin, *A Good Cause to Publish?*. London: BLD Group Ltd, 1996.

Coxall, W. N., and L. Robins, *Contemporary British Politics*. London: Macmillan, 1994.

Dunleavy, Patrick and Stuart Weir, 'It's All Over for the Old Constitution', *Independent*, 30 May, 1995.

Grant, Wyn, *Pressure Groups, Politics and Democracy in Britain*, 2nd edn. Hemel Hempstead: Harvester, 1995.

Healey, John, *Cause and Effect*. London: NCVO Publications, 1991.

Henley Centre/NCVO Third Sector Foresight, Conference Papers 1997.

Hudson, Mike, *Managing Without Profit*. London: Penguin Books, 1995.

Hull, W. and S. Weir, *The Untouchables*. London: Democratic Audit and the Scarman Trust, 1996.

Kendall, J. and M. Knapp, *The Voluntary Sector in the UK*. Manchester: Manchester University Press, 1996.

Knight, Barry, *Voluntary Action*. London: HMSO, 1993.

Marr, Andrew, *Ruling Britannia: The Failure and Future of British Democracy*. London: Penguin Books, 1995.

Mulgan, Geoff, and Charles Landry, *The Other Invisible Hand: Remaking Charity for the 21st Century*. London: Demos, 1995.

Lord Nathan (Chair), *Effectiveness and the Voluntary Sector: Report of a Working Party*. London: NCVO Publications, 1990.

NCVO, *Meeting the Challenge of Change: Voluntary Action into the 21st Century*, a report of the Commission on the Future of the Voluntary Sector. London: NCVO Publications, 1996a.

Hems, Les, and Andrew Passey, *The UK Voluntary Sector Statistical Almanac 1996*. London: NCVO Publications, 1996.

NCVO briefing paper. London: NCVO Publications.

Lord Nolan (Chair), *Standards in Public Life: First Report of the Committee on Standards in Public Life*. London: HMSO1995,.

Opinion Leader Research Survey, April 1994 (unpublished).

Parminter, Kate, cited in *The Observer*, 16 March 1997.
Parsons, Wayne, *Public Policy: An Introduction to the Theory and Practice of Policy Analysis*. London: Edward Elger, 1995.

Perri 6, *Restricting the Freedom of Speech of Charities: Do the Rationales Stand Up?* London: Demos, 1994.

Richardson, J., *Purchase of Service Contracting*. London: NCVO Publications, 1995.

Rose, Chris, cited in *The Observer*, 16 March 1997.

Seyd, Patrick, and Paul Whiteley, 'Labour and Conservative Party Members', *Parliamentary Affairs, A Journal of Comparative Politics*, Vol.48, No.3, July. Oxford: Oxford University Press, 1995.

Social Trends 1996. London: HMSO.

Appendix 5: Further Reading

GENERAL

Baggot, Rob, *Pressure Groups Today*. Manchester: Manchester University Press, 1995.
Comprehensive account of academic theories on pressure groups.

Bruce, Ian, *Meeting Need: Successful Charity Marketing*. Hemel Hempstead: Institute of Chartered Secretaries and Administrators, 1994.
Applies marketing concepts to the development of a campaign and includes case studies.

Hutt, Jane, *Opening the Town Hall Door*. London: NCVO Publications, 1990.
Guide to campaigning and advocacy on local authority issues - out of print.

Waldegrave, William, Charles Secrett, Peter Bazalgette, Adam Gaines and Kate Parminter, *Pressure Group Politics in Modern Britain*. London: Social Market Foundation, 1996.

CAMPAIGNING

Bird, Polly, *How to Run a Local Campaign: A Step-by-step Manual for Organisers*. Plymouth: Northcote House, 1989.
Blow-by-blow account of how to run a local campaign with practical examples. Aimed at small community groups.

Lattimer, Mark, *The Campaigners Handbook*. London: Directory of Social Change, 1994.
A comprehensive, general guide to campaigning.

Wilson, Des, with Leighton Andrews, *The A to Z of Public Advocacy*. London: Hawksmere, 1993.

Dubs, Alf, *Lobbying: An Insider's Guide to the Parliamentary Process*. London: Pluto

Parliamentary lobbying

Dubs, Alf, *Lobbying: An Insider's Guide to the Parliamentary Process.* London: Pluto Press, 1988.
One of the best and clearest guides on everything related to parliamentary procedure by a former Labour MP who is now a member of the House of Lords, sadly now out of print.

Miller, *Lobbying Government: Understanding and Influencing the Corridors of Power.* Oxford: Basil Blackwell, 1987.
A comprehensive, practical and well-informed work which deals with the operation of government at all levels. Written by a leading commercial lobbyist.